The Black Book of

PERSUASION

23 principles that move your will

Alex Llantada

The Black Book of
PERSUASION

23 principles that move your will

Title of the Book: *The Black Book of Persuasion:*
23 principles that move your will

Content

With heartfelt thanks to my loved ones.

Prologue

As a public image consultant, I have been an ongoing student and practitioner of propaganda. In fact, all public image consultants are propagandists par excellence, since this is the science we resort to whenever we want to arouse emotions in the audience and move them toward our customers' objectives. Propaganda is used to multiply, induce, incite, and spread the word to create an awareness of a given thing and to awaken emotions regarding that product, service or political party. For what? The goal is always to persuade!

At the College of Public Image, I always provide all my students with the following definition of propaganda, which is "the action and effect of publicizing something to win over followers and persuade them." Persuading is to move, to induce, to incite, to provoke, or even to force someone to do or believe something. This book can help you get what you want.

The phenomenon of persuasion is not just to be studied but used to get results through our actions. These actions are described in *The Black Book of Persuasion* and transformed into principles that Alex Llantada gave a name and surname, so we can become familiar with them and use that knowledge to our advantage or shield us from its power.

Madame de Staël, the celebrated adversary of Napoleon, said: "The intelligent can be convinced; the foolish persuaded." Notice that the word persuasion has a somewhat negative emotional connotation. We think that those who persuade, manipulate, and stack the cards in their favor, and this is only too true, although not necessarily in a negative way. I think that one of Llantada's major contributions is that he separates us from the bad vibes associated with the word "persuasion." In fact, he teaches us to understand the word, to use it, to embrace and respect it, and even to love it.

Some great leaders have used these principles. Ancient wise men, such as Sun Tzu or Renaissance philosopher Machiavelli have taught these techniques. Contemporary authors such as Dale Carnegie and Robert Greene have reconsidered the subject, creating high-value bestsellers. You now have in your hands a book that brings them all together and introduces you in a pleasant and straightforward fashion to the fascinating world of persuasion.

There are few books like this one. It is up to you to decide whether to keep on reading or to stay unaware. I can assure you that this book will help you achieve your goals and, by the way, this foreword was written bearing in mind many of the principles you will find in this book.

Alvaro Gordoa

INTRODUCTION

All my life I was at the mercy of invisible manipulations until I found in an old notebook with handwritten notes by my father, a phrase that refers to "the principles of sales". It was so simple and yet so powerful that it opened my eyes and understanding.

This notebook included some case studies from Harvard that spoke of "The Principle of Reciprocity." Its discovery represented only the beginning of extensive research in books and speeches written by various experts in sales, social psychology and persuasion. So, what is this Principle of Reciprocity? It is very simple; it is what is perceived when a person does something for you or gives you something, for instance, a beautiful pen. Who has not felt, consciously or subconsciously, indebted in a situation like this?

If we cast our minds back, we can realize of have been victims of this principle by being enticed to do things we might not have wanted to do. As a child, I accompanied my mother on an adventure called "time-share," a marketing gimmick that begins by offering a free breakfast and as a prize an all-expense paid trip to Cancun. Once there, after announcing the "prize," a large group of people screamed and shout, toasting to our new acquisition. Distressed, my mom asked: What did I supposedly just buy? With this trick and some others, people are pushed to accept an awful and very expensive lifetime contract. Many guests are forced to sign and "purchase" an apartment that they may only use twice a year, after all the false attention, gifts, and announcements from the top echelon about the alleged purchase decision. This type of experience just serves as an example of why we must become familiar with the principles of persuasion. Although I know you are thinking: "This will not happen to me." Don´t be so sure!

My father's notebook was not the only trigger that launched me into research about the psychological make-up of the human being, and a genuine desire to answer: What leads me do something?

A philosophy professor made me think about the following question: "Are human beings free?" After a series of bickering and reviewing the Kantian philosophy, structuralism, and others which I do not remember, my professor, my colleagues and I concluded that no, we are not free. Everyone influences us in some way; indeed, there are companies and institutions devoted specifically to persuade us to do something that we do not necessarily want to do. This situation is not distant to our inner circle. You and I influence the world and you and I, in turn, are influenced by others, not just by vendors, political parties or advertising agencies, but also by spouses, children, priests, and teachers, all of whom apply these powerful principles, some of them unknowingly.

It was by chance (or fate) that I discovered Robert B. Cialdini, a famous author in the 1980's, who wrote about some principles regarding the science of persuasion. I read one of his very illustrative examples: a social psychologist surveyed the residents of an area asking them what they would do if invited to utilize three hours of their time to raise funds for a cancer foundation. They all said they would gladly accept (it looked good in the survey, and they would not be considered selfish by the interviewer). To their surprise, and just after accepting on paper to help, they were asked to do so. The fact is that just by agreeing to the terms of the first question on, they felt compelled to accept because of something called "The Principle of Consistency."

After researching without much luck but with greater intentionality, I found that several studies in social psychology support the ideas I discovered, some heuristically, others through investigation, and I included them in this work as proven principles established by many scientific experiments and by my personal experience.

My promise is that after reading this book, you will be able to know how to discern all the manipulations (some good, some bad, and some necessary) you face every day. The advertisement that claims that a given brand of yogurt supports children with certain disabilities (Principle of Blackmail, Principle of the Unconscious, Principle of Association). The political candidate who makes us believe that if we had voted for him, we would better off (Principle of Antagonism, Principle of Consistency, and Principle of Contrast). The priest who tells a parable (Principle of Metaphor). When we go to a place, even if it is full and must wait for a long time to be seated (Principle of Social Acceptance).

In brief, I will explain all the possible situations you may face and are conditioned and influenced to act. I have named the situations, so it is easy to identify and understand them. These will also allow you to apply this knowledge in a reverse process, for your convenience. Of course, an individual's code of ethics shall rule over the proper use of this power.

The pistol is now loaded, and I hand it to you. Only you will know if you use it in self-defense, to save lives, or to abuse others. Without a doubt, its original nature does not change; a shot bullet will always pierce.

1. **THE PRINCIPLE OF RECIPROCITY:** *What is given will be received back.* If you get something you value, you will feel a desire to respond with something of equal or greater value.

2. **THE PRINCIPLE OF CONTRAST:** *White seems whiter on a black background.* We will perceive the opposite characteristics of two items by placing them next to each other. It becomes easier for us to notice the differences between them, thus making it quicker for us to decide.

3. **THE PRINCIPLE OF AFFINITY:** *I like him/her. Why not?* If someone that you honestly trust and like asks for something, you may feel inclined to give it to him or her.

4. THE PRINCIPLE OF EXPECTATION: *What you expect will be.* What you assume about someone else will become real, for better or for worse. Consciously or subconsciously, our expectations are at play.

5. THE PRINCIPLE OF ASSOCIATION: *If James Bond uses it, then it must be good.* Goods and services are associated with the people who use or recommend them. If we think something positive or negative of that individual, we will associate it.

6. THE PRINCIPLE OF CONSISTENCY: *If I said so, I would do so.* If a claim has been made in front of a witness or where there is evidence, it will tend to be consistent and congruent with what was said in the presence of the people who read or heard what was said. If you believe that something is good or bad, you tend to justify your actions along these lines.

7. THE PRINCIPLE OF SCARCITY: *If there are only a few of them, they will be more expensive.* This is the law of supply and demand. When an item is thought to be scarce, people believe that it is worthwhile. If the supply of that item is abundant and anyone can have it, then the item is worth less.

8. THE PRINCIPLE OF AUTHORITY: *I obey the doctor's instructions.* We tend to follow the instructions of someone who is considered to be an authority to unimaginable extremes.

9. THE PRINCIPLE OF COERCION: *If you don't do it, you'll pay.* When someone threatens to take negative action if the other party does something or stops doing something, conditioning for fear will lead to a change in behavior.

10. THE PRINCIPLE OF ATTRACTIVENESS: *If someone is appealing, I will agree.* If someone or something is perceived to be attractive or beautiful, there is a greater chance for having agreed to what is being requested.

11. **THE PRINCIPLE OF POWER:** *If you give me power, I will follow.* If a person makes you believe that thanks to his/her power you will achieve certain benefits, such as: sexual favors; love; political, economic, or spiritual influence; you will follow him/her.

12. **THE PRINCIPLE OF INCENTIVES:** *You can have this if you do this.* Humans react to incentives, and they will do everything possible to satisfy their personal interests.

13. **THE PRINCIPLE OF SUBCONSCIOUS:** *Take charge of my dreams.* The unconscious mind acts in conjunction with the conscious mind, with the difference that people do not realize it is the submerged part of the iceberg. It guides the mostly hidden aspects of peoples' will.

14. **THE PRINCIPLE OF ANTAGONISM:** *Join me against him.* When there is an enemy, real or imaginary, against whom to fight, an individual will join the group and focus on a common goal. Being against something hooks everyone; it is even a must in the survival of species.

15. **THE PRINCIPLE OF PRECEDENT:** *I believe it because it has already happened.* We believe that something existed or worked in the past will probably happen and work again.

16. **THE PRINCIPLE OF WRITTEN EXPRESSION:** *If it is written, it is God's word.* What is written is more powerful than what is left unrecorded.

17. **THE PRINCIPLE OF FAITH:** *Believe me, and I will give you a purpose.* People are influenced by faith and trust. People will follow you if they believe in a larger sublime power.

18. **THE PRINCIPLE OF METAPHOR:** *If I say heart, understand love.* The reality is hard and cruel, so an indirect idea (metaphor) is easier to understand.

19. **THE PRINCIPLE OF THE UNEXPECTED:** *What a pleasant surprise, I was not expecting it!* What is unexpected may be charming and convincing.

20. **THE PRINCIPLE OF PRAISE:** *You are so intelligent!* We are all vulnerable to flattery, and it is hard to resist.

21. **THE PRINCIPLE OF SOCIAL ACCEPTANCE:** *It must be good if so many like it.* The more people think or do something in common, the more that influences others to believe it is right or acceptable.

22. **THE PRINCIPLE OF SIMPLICITY:** *I like you because I understand you.* What is stated in an uncomplicated way will be pleasant and more influential.

23. **THE PRINCIPLE OF I AM:** *We are all one.* We all share the same spirit and we are all one. If we re-member this truth, we will recognize ourselves in each other and will not need any other persuasion principle.

The most compelling personalities in history have applied more than one of these principles to achieve their goals, but they are not the only ones who have done this. All politicians, religious figures, marketers, public image consultants, advertisers, you, and I, sometimes do things knowingly, but most of the time unknowingly. Who has not coerced a partner or a spouse? Who has not bought something expensive just because it is not very commonplace? Who has not been the victim of an attractive person by agreeing to do something that would not do otherwise?

These principles are so powerful that it is worthwhile analyzing them for a deeper understanding. Schools and universities should teach this as part of basic training for all students: Becoming familiar with these principles and knowing how to apply them would help all of us achieve a higher level of performance in our professional and personal lives.

It is important to be forewarned so we do not become victims of ill-intentioned third-party manipulation; the only way to prevent this is by understanding the Principles of Persuasion. Knowing what makes the *wheels spin* will help you not only defend yourself against the influence of others, but also will show you how to use this power in your favor.

Alex Llantada

1. PRINCIPLE OF RECIPROCITY
What is given will be received back

"For every action, there is an equal and opposite reaction."
Isaac Newton

If you receive something you value, you will find yourself willing to give something of a similar or larger value in return.

Life is like a boomerang. What you do will be done to you and what you do will come back to you for better or for worse (1).

It is said that once upon a time, a poor Scottish farmer heard a cry coming from a pond. Coming closer, he found a young boy drowning in the mud and manure. Without hesitation, he saved him from a terrible death. The next day, a wealthy man knocked at his door: he was the father the boy he had saved the day before. As a gesture of gratitude, the man offered the farmer to pay for his son's college education at the best university. Many years later, the son of the wealthy man got pneumonia, and thanks to Alexander Fleming, his life was saved. Fleming was the son of the farmer who had graduated from St. Mary's Medicine School in London and had discovered penicillin. By the way, the name of the son of the wealthy man was Winston Churchill. Favors pay back favors.

The principal of reciprocity says that for everything given, something will be received in return. An action produces an effect. In physics, this principle states that for every action, there is an equal and opposite reaction.

In cultural anthropology, the term reciprocity refers to the exchange of goods and labor. It is the most common interaction in those societies that are not in the buying-selling of goods and services (2).

Reciprocity can be found in all cultures since ancient times. We can use the Incas and other pre-Hispanic cultures as an example. They did not have currencies or monies. They had to give something in return for a good or service received. Reciprocity was not required but requested. This principle of reciprocity is present in our daily lives in many ways.

I already gave something to you; now it is your turn
While walking down the street suddenly a girl puts a "happy face" sticker on your jacket. Surprised and annoyed, you may feel obligated to give her a coin. The feeling is present even if you decide not to do it. This happens very often in public places of several cultures. In the United States, the religious group Hare Krishna was famous for putting flowers on the lapel of passersby and this gesture caught by surprise the person receiving the flowers, who in return gave money. This method was overused and lost its effectiveness.

Social interactions and reciprocity are closely related. Psychological studies show, for instance, that waiters who smile at their customers get better tips than those who are not so friendly. When a smile is given, a tip is received in return (3).

Requests for contributions to charities are often accompanied by small gifts. Apparently, charity organizations know that this increases the propensity to donate. In general, it is likely to generate feelings that make people feel obligated to pay for the psychological debt with a donation (4).

In sales, a significant example of reciprocity is the use of free samples. In supermarkets, customers often try out small amounts of a free product. Many people find it difficult to accept the samples a smiling demonstrator doles out without buying anything in return. Other people buy the product even if they do not like it very much (4).

The normative power of reciprocity also has a substantial impact on social policy issues. Public opinion approves or disapproves any government decision, taking into consideration the rewards, independently of how these decisions will affect society and to what extent (5).

Eye for an Eye
Reciprocity is not exclusive to material aspects but is also related to moral order and interpersonal relationships. It is known as "The Golden Rule" or ethic of reciprocity; a moral maxim or principle of altruism found in many cultures and religions, suggesting that it is related to basic human nature.

The act of paying back a favor or a donation is well understood in all philosophies and religions. Confucius, for example, explains: "When you cultivate most of the principles of nature and hold to the principle of reciprocity, you are not far off the right path. Do not do unto others what you do not want others to do unto you". In Buddhism, this is known as a karmic law of cause and effect. Conversely, we know it as the law of retaliation from Late Latin *retaliare* "pay back in kind".

Reciprocity in humans is essential for the survival of the species. It is an almost automatic mechanism involving evolution and civility. When wasted or ignored, the result may only turn against us in the form of hatred or apathy. Give and you´ll receive in return (often) even more than what you gave.

"Cause and effect, means and ends, seed and fruit cannot be severed; for the effect already blooms in the cause, the end preexists in the means, the fruit in the seed."
Ralph Waldo Emerson

2. PRINCIPLE OF CONTRAST
White seems whiter on a black background

"Disease makes health pleasant and good; hunger- satiety;
Weariness- rest".
Heraclitus

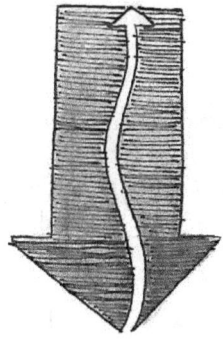

When comparing two items with opposite characteristics against each other, it is easier to notice their differences and decide.

Contrast is the opposition of figures, situations, fortune, customs, benevolence, beauty, or credulity. Contrast is what allows us to weigh a reality by presenting it with an apparent opposite: light-dark, day-night, low-high, large-small, etc., but also generated with elements that do not have a binary relation as beauty-kindness, price-quality, classic-innovator and any other that you can think.

Voltaire said: "It is not the same as two things that contrast with being contradictory. It is not contradictory that the pope should have been worshiped in Rome and burned in London on the same

19

day, and that while they called him vice God in Italy, he would cross the streets of Moscow represented by a pig figure to amuse Peter the Great.

Muhammad, whom half the world places at the right hand of God, is also regarded as an impostor by the other half of the inhabitants of the Earth. Such contrasts reflect a relationship that goes beyond the immediate and apparent because different beliefs, lifestyles, interests, personalities, and conceptual frameworks come into play.

Contradictory, for example, is to want to die when you are alive, to hate a loved one or to kill someone who gives you food as in the case of nature. The contradictory always contrasts, but what contrasts is not always contradictory." (6)

It is well known that opposites generate contrast, but the duality of *yin-yang* explains that it is all part of the whole, and if white is the presence of all colors, black is the absence of them. The devil himself, synonymous with evil, was named at first by God as *Luzbelle* or Beautiful-Light. The enlightened Greek philosopher Heraclitus, known as "The Obscure One from Ephesus," had a very positive approach to life: "It is by disease that health is pleasant, by evil that good is pleasant, by hunger satiety, by weariness rest."

White looks brighter on a black background. When two things are compared, and are opposites of each other, it is easier to notice the difference and then decide for yourself.

Lighting the darkness of death

Salvador Dali once said: "My maternal grandmother, Ana, who was ninety years, fell into a kind of languid madness after the death of one of her daughters. She took refuge in her past and evoked abundant details of the episodes of her otherwise happy life. She often spoke in verse and recited Gongora. For her, we were all strangers. Her only contact with reality was while having meals, and she would get excited about meringues. An hour before her death, she sat up in bed and said, 'My grandson will be the most important Catalan painter ever.' Then she fell asleep and never woke up again. The imminence of death makes us clairvoyants." (7)

This brief Dali anecdote feeds of contrast: "Extrasensory perception" allows us to capture future events, which traditionally are associated with wisdom, and break with the scheme of unreality, such as the one in which the old woman lived. Amid everyday absurdities and languid madness, a spark of inspiration emerges, making the message more noticeable and even better than if it came from someone who was usually lucid, and not just before dying.

Light in darkness and the prophecy that is truly out of this world is taken as credible and real due to contrast.

For ten dollars more

Merchandising (the part of marketing that aims to increase profitability at the point of sale), uses this practice to present contrasting concepts for objects in showcases, and window displays. For example, in the department that sells pens, several items are on display, but on the top shelf, coincidentally, we find an ugly or cheap pen on sale. Next to this pen on sale, there is a strikingly attractive pen at a much higher price. Some 63% of the consumers will purchase the nicer pen even if it has a higher price tag. The lower priced ugly pen enhances the attractiveness of the expensive one. The remaining 37% buy the cheap pen or another product in the mid-range. (8)

Contrast law is also intelligently applied in fast food hamburgers. When you order and the attendant offers you to add bacon or increase the size of potatoes or soda for a minimal extra amount of money, the low price will most likely cause you to accept the offer. The owners of the chain become millionaires with economies of scale, because the 10% difference in price means more than 30%

in profit. The same thing happens when a guy buys a suit and they offer him a tie. It looks so cheap compared to the price of the suit, that he accepts the bargain.

Politicians tend to be experts in contrasting their strengths with the weaknesses of their adversaries. The opponents of the ruling party point to low investments, zero growth, and problems of insecurity. On the other hand, the ruling party highlights the lack of experience of new candidates and announces campaigns to punish the corruption of past administrations, for instance. During the Cuban revolution, Fidel Castro defeated former dictator Fulgencio Batista with the promise that he was headed toward democracy. However, Castro's government eventually became one of the most solid dictatorships in modern history.

We are always comparing ourselves to others, and it is part of the inherent characteristic of our ego. Jealousy and envy have roots in this feature. The animal kingdom also compares and discriminates to eliminate what is poisonous or not, fertile, or sterile, suitable or not. Religions also use comparisons to help us distinguish between good and evil.

Black and white psyche

In social psychology, the effect of contrast refers to the influence of previous stimuli in the evaluation or judgment of new ones. Some experiments performed on this principle are:

- Social judgment: Someone may appear meaner or kinder when compared to someone else (DiVesta, 1961; Harvey & Sherif, 1957).
- Estimates of weight: Something feels heavier after previously carrying something lighter (Sherif, Taub, & Hovland, 1958).
- Ratings of the attractiveness of women: A woman is more beautiful when contrasted (Kerick & Gutierres, 1980).
- Studies of visual perception: White seems whiter on a black background (Helson, 1964).

- Judgments in interviews: A professional seems more apt if interviewed after a session with a weak candidate (Kopelman, 1975; Carlson, 1970).

These experiments studied the contrast between two stimuli and the result in all cases revealed that the comparison of two opposite items created the perception that one of them is better or more intense.

Dress in yellow and your teeth will look whiter than ever. Sit next to an ugly person, and you will look beautiful. Compare yourself to someone with less money, and you will feel rich. The fastest way to make you feel better is by using the contrast principle.

"There are dark shadows on the earth, but its lights are stronger in the contrast."
Charles Dickens

3. PRINCIPLE OF AFFINITY
I like him/her. Why not?

" If you could win over a man for your cause, first convince him that you are his sincere friend."
Abraham Lincoln

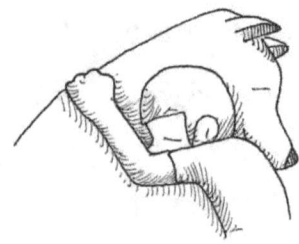

If someone you appreciate or feel is genuinely interested in you requests a favor, you will feel obliged to agree or accept.

Lewis Carroll was traveling in a train car, and sitting next to him was a woman with her daughter, who was reading *Alice in Wonderland*. When the girl closed the book, he began to talk to her about the story, and the mother joined the conversation. Without knowing that he was the author of the book, the woman commented: "Isn't it sad what happened to Mr. Carroll? He lost his mind, did you know that?" "Really?" replied the author, "I had no idea." She answered: "I can assure you that a credible source told me so!"

Before saying goodbye, Carroll got permission to send a gift to the girl, who days later received a copy of the book "*Through the Looking-Glass, and What Alice Found There*" with the following dedication: "From the author, as a souvenir of an enjoyable trip." The writer placed a higher value on the girl's admiration of his work than her mother´s comment. He chatted happily, enjoyed their company, and despite being a successful and famous man, still took the trouble to send a gift to a little girl; affinity persuades anybody.

Please buy one from me!

It is hard to say "no" to a friend who asks us for a favor. It is not easy to say "no" to someone we like. Herbert Spencer explained this: "Ultimately, opinions are determined by feelings, not by intellect." Not in vain, emotions determine shopping spree purchases, which generate 76% of sales in grocery stores and 59% in department stores. They appeal to emotions and not to reason, which is the key to shopping, and sellers are always searching to create pleasant shopping experiences.

Getting to the heart of a potential customer is the key to developing different business concepts. "If I like you, I trust you, and you like me." This is the underlying message of music, smiles, and kindness, although it is true that some salespeople behind the cash registers at stores don´t seem to understand this yet.

Thus, multi-level companies have their roots in this concept. Their representatives sell different products (shoes, containers, juice with magical properties, electronic devices, and investment funds) to friends and relatives. The implicit message: "If my friend recommends it, has to be good. He would not lie to me nor would he recommend a defective product." Some sects and religious and civil organizations function in the same way. People show their friendship and then accept many things they have been offered. The message has a strong effect: "If my friends offer it to me, it is because it is to the best of my interests."

The law of affinity is part the origin of life itself. It is the seed of any family, community, and country. It is what creates links, institutions, and guilds, ranging from having the same nationality to professing the same religion or preferring the same sports team. The law of affinity is the silent pact that allows us to trust other members of a group. It is the programmed conviction that a friend has a characteristic or a skill that I too should learn or develop.

Although you can generate artificial affinity, empathy works when it is authentic. Companies and business systems use this law to improve their sales, but they do not cheat people, which would be impossible in the long term. What they do is take advantage of the existing sympathy in society to promote their products immediately. Salespeople use this principle to sell more using their personal qualities for approaching consumers and establishing rapport with them.

Emotional intelligence; condition of affinity
It is proven that people who live longer, are happier, earn more money, last longer married, and feel successful, are those that generate high empathy. After all, the word "friend" means "close to me." A genuine interest in people allows you to make friends quickly. That is the thesis Dale Carnegie sets forth in his book *How to Make Friends and Influence People*. Let us look at a general overview of this valuable work:

Part 1: Fundamental techniques for dealing with people
- Do not criticize them, do not condemn them, do not complain.
- Flatter people in a sincere and honest way.
- Make them want something intensely.

Part 2: Six ways to make people like you
- Show a genuine interest in others.
- Always smile.
- Remember that the name of a person sounds good in any language.
- Be a good "listener" by encouraging people to talk about themselves. Always speak to them about topics that interest them.
- Always make the other person feel you care about them and do this sincerely.

Part 3: Make people think like you

- The only way to get out of a disagreement is to avoid it.
- Show respect for the opinions of the other person, never say: "You are wrong."
- If you are wrong, admit it immediately and emphasize the fact that it was an honest mistake.
- Speak in a friendly way.
- Say something so that the other person will say "yes" immediately.
- Let the other party do most of the talking.
- Make them believe that the idea you want to develop is their own.
- Try to see things from the perspective of the other side in a sincere way.
- Try to identify with their ideas and wishes.

Part 4: Be a leader. How to change people without offending them and causing resistance

The functions of a leader often include changing the attitudes and behavior of others. To do this:

- Start with a sincere compliment.
- In an indirect fashion; make them aware of their mistake.
- Talk about your mistakes before mentioning theirs.
- Ask questions instead of giving direct orders.
- Give them the opportunity not to feel embarrassed.
- Praise any improvement noted in their behavior.
- Try to identify with their ideas and wishes.
- Give them a good reputation, so they feel committed to meet such high expectations.
- Encourage people and make them understand that mistakes are easy to correct and overcome.
- Make them feel happy by doing what you suggested needed to be done.

Does empathy really work?

Burt Swersey had a great idea when he read a study by Bell Labs in which engineering researchers mentioned that they attributed their success to their emotional intelligence and not to their technical skills. That inspired Swersey to try something different with his students at the Rensselaer Polytechnic Institute.

At the beginning of the class, he talked about the Bell Labs study and the "five secrets of success": affinity, empathy, persuasion, cooperation, and consensus building. Then he announced that instead of spending their first-day reviewing basic engineering concepts, they would conduct a learning lab on the five secrets.

"How would you go about establishing rapport with someone you don't know?" Swersey asked. By asking this question, he started a vigorous discussion not related to engineering at all. The students developed empathy and affinity by going through the exercises of persuasion, cooperation, and consensus building. At the end of the class, the students devoted 3 minutes to decide which was the best ice cream in the world and why.

What was the result of this little social experiment? "The students turned out to be the best teams I have had in years of introduction to engineering design," said Swersey. "Not only did they work together, but they were also better than my previous students. They produced innovative and hugely ambitious artifacts. I attribute much of the success to the time we spent on the five secrets". Swersey´s experiment addressed a major problem of organizations concerned about highly educated experts lacking leadership skills.

This approach to developing a group's cohesion can be found more and more in professional academics, such as the Harvard Business School and the Sloan School of Management. "Nowadays syllabi are based more on the concept of team-work." Kim goes on to explain: "It is a response to the criticism of companies where they say that business managers are very well prepared as individuals, but need to learn to work together in teams as well" (9).

Teamwork always requires the application of the principle of affinity: only members of the group can be mutually persuaded to generate synergies. The sum of intelligence is the result of social skills experience and reflects three types of neurons that interact with each other: mirror, fusiform and oscillatory. The first one allows us to monitor other people's emotions, what is their state of mind? The second one involves intuition, "Do I trust them?" The last one allows us to tune in with people, physically, coordinating with each other; for instance, when musicians play in an orchestra.

Affinity drives better relationships, increases sales and productivity in the workplace, and improves communication in any relationship. Honesty is required for affinity to work: always be truthful and sincere, faked affinity never works, be the real Mc Coy!!

"Affinity is a unique, discreet and independent feeling. You can be miles away, but you can guess people's emotions by their way of talking, writing, walking, breathing ..."
Artur Da Távola

4. PRINCIPLE OF EXPECTATION
What you expect will be

"Higher expectations are the key to achieving success."
Sam Walton

What you assume of someone else, will come true, for better or for worse. Consciously or unconsciously, our expectations are met.

Robert Kearns, a modest university professor, revolutionized the automotive industry in the United States thanks to a top of the line invention, but he also embarked on a daunting crusade against international automobile companies to recognize his invention.

After his design and patent had been brazenly stolen, the professor decided not to surrender to the most important industries in Detroit. The inventor of the intermittent windshield wiper mechanism sued two huge automobile companies demanding payment for his invention, and he succeeded (10). Kearns's mother always told him: "You will always achieve what you want. You have what it takes to get there." He believed in this. Others believed in him.

The principle of expectation to succeed was a positive reinforcement in his early life.

Cook and cure

Imagine that you are a terrible cook, but your partner thinks that you cook wonderfully because someone said so. Your mother also made the comment that you are great chef in a recent chat at a restaurant. Your partner asks you to prepare a delicious recipe his family loves. What would you do? Well, make a good dish! You will try at all costs to comply with peoples' expectations.

The "placebo effect" is another example of the principle of expectation. Scientists have known for a long time that if a patient is given a pill and is told that it is medicine (for example, for a headache), it is very likely that the person will feel relief just by believing this to be the case. A similar effect occurs with hypochondriacs: if someone claims to have the avian flu and sneezes, they will begin to feel strange symptoms. They will meet their expectations in whole or in part.

Even when there is no light, much is expected of me

George Elton Mayo is very famous in the field of organizational behavior, and in 1928 he was invited to participate in a practical research study on productivity in a factory. He conducted a series of experiments using different conditions: lighting, noise, fatigue, and other factors related to the workplace. He asked for the removal of all previously implemented workplace improvements: all scheduled breaks, lighting, free lunches, and any other conditions associated with an increase in productivity were suspended. The outcome was unexpected: production did not slow down, quite the contrary, it increased.

The outcome was the result of persuading workers to collaborate and convincing them of the relevance of the experiment. The elevated expectations vested in them and the ensuing compliments worked as motivating forces.

Workers were persuaded to collaborate and were convinced of the relevance of the experiment. They were clearly motivated by feeling flattered and knowing what was expected of them (11).

The most beautiful woman in the world

Pygmalion was a very talented sculptor in ancient Greece, who would spend hours carving beautiful ivory statues. One day he chose a large, beautiful piece of ivory, and worked diligently on it, chiseling, and hammering, and he fell in love with the maiden sculpture he was creating. After finishing his work, he constantly prayed to the gods to give life to his sculpture, convinced that there would never be such a beautiful woman in the world. He sought with such fervor and passion for the gods to grant his wish that the sculpture turned into a woman of flesh and blood.

The Pygmalion effect is not only mythological: people will achieve their purposes if they believe they can do so. The self-fulfilling prophecy acts as an expectation that incites people to act in a way that allows things to turn into reality.

Psychology defines the Pygmalion effect, also known as the self-fulfilling prophecy, as an expectation or prediction which will become a reality for those who see it coming, making the unconscious work in a way consistent with what has been foreseen.

How is it that everything becomes a reality?

By communicating in a positive manner, we increase the probabilities of positively influencing others and helping them to adapt their behavior to ours.

It is an interesting phenomenon because individuals are rarely aware of the fact that their own expectations influence others' behavior. Not in vain did social researchers Rosenthal and Jacobson state, "Teacher expectations and forecasts affect student performance." These two social researchers analyzed the importance of beliefs and school performance results and determined that the highest expectations led to the most rewarding outcomes (12).

Henry Ford stated, "No matter whether you think you can or cannot, you are right," and this is a perfect quote to illustrate the principle of expectation.

Jane Elliot performed an experiment about discrimination of blue over brown eyes. She divided a third-grade classroom into two groups according to their eye color. The first day the blue-eyed kids were treated as superior, and the brown-eyed ones were considered less intelligent and with lower learning capabilities. On the second day, roles were switched, and the brown-eyed children were found to be superior and their blue-eyed counterparts were treated as inferior.

Every day she tested the children by giving spelling exams to the students in the two groups. The students who were treated as superior achieved higher scores and vice versa (13).

Feldman and Prohaska performed another experiment to study the effect of expectations of students from their professors. According to this study, they demonstrated that when a student is led to believe that a teacher is "good" (by gossip or false rumors), the student will think that the teacher is "effective". Students demonstrated a higher level of engagement, expressed even in their body language: they tend to lean closer to the teacher and establish more eye contact. On the other hand, to the contrary, the rumor that a teacher is bad produced an adverse effect. Interesting enough, the students' performance was also influenced by expectations provoked.

Expect the best of others, and you will get it. Expect the best of yourself, and your dreams will come true. To the contrary, if you expect the worst, your nightmares will be waiting sat on your favorite couch when you come home from work.

"Expect that people are better than what they are, and this will help them turn into someone better. Do not feel disappointed if they do not achieve this. It will help them to keep on trying".
Merry Browne

5. PRINCIPLE OF ASSOCIATION
If James Bond uses it,
then it must be good

-*"Q, I will take the Aston Martin to go for a ride ..."*
-*"Be careful, 007! We just give it a coat of paint".*
The Living Daylight, 1987

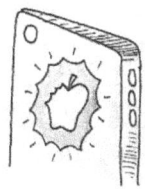

Goods and services are associated with the people who use or recommend them. If we think something positive or negative of that individual, we will associate it.

Pablo Picasso was laying down under the sun at a beach in Southern France when a boy approached him with a piece of paper in his hand asking the artist to draw something for him. Picasso realized that the kid's parent had sent him to get a small piece of art for free.

Picasso got rid of the piece of paper and put his signature on the child's back. A few days later, during a small gathering, he narrated his experience to some of his friends. He said to them giggling "I wonder if they have given him a bath!" (14).

The famous pieces of an artist are related to his fame, and in this sense, his pieces can be considered as "good," "bad," "valuable" or "cheap." If something is not worthy, it will be due to the reputation of its creator.

I am famous, and I recommend it

People rarely question the connotations that can merge from association. How many ads have we seen involving popular figures from show business? It is hard to believe that a TV actress' opinion about health issues is trustworthy. Certainly, she is being paid to make public advertisements. The audience believes her, and they believe that the product she endorses works and that consumers will purchase these products. Fashion is founded on this same principle. When a well-known designer proposes something incredible, high-income consumers will follow his lead, wearing his creations, and then the middle class supports, forming a chain of association.

Sometimes inspirations come about in just the opposite way. A trendsetter can be inspired by lower socioeconomic levels, when something ridiculous or considered to be in bad taste turns into something desirable, moving on from kitsch to chic. For instance, nowadays jeans can be quite expensive when originally the garments were used by blue-collar workers. Tequila is another example. It was traditionally considered to be a cheap drink but now is a sophisticated international one. So, something inexpensive can become *cool* just by a chain of association.

Election times

Politicians are the kingpins of association, especially when they are campaigning. If they are handsome, we will see them greeting women warmly to enhance the association, and attractive or not; they will snuggle hold babies until their arms get swollen. They will be surrounded by famous personalities: beautiful actresses and well-known writers, who will make them look more attractive and intelligent. They will become solidary with popular causes, and try to be associated with anyone who represents a characteristic they need. They know they need fame and therefore want to be seen with famous people. Their only objective is to improve their own public image.

As voters, we like to think that the opinions of the media do not influence us. We like to believe that we are critical thinkers, well-informed and with a good sense of self-criticism. However, Brian Knight and Chug Fang Chiang, researchers at the University of Brown, published a study in the Review of Economic Studies, that there is a significant effect on voters thanks to the influence the media has.

The results of this study indicate that they are more likely to support a candidate after he has been endorsed by a newspaper. This is quite evident, but the researchers also found out that potential voters take into consideration the political inclination of the press: for instance, support of a leftist candidate by a leftist-leaning newspaper is seen as less credible than if he were backed by a neutral or conservative newspaper. Politicians of the world: now you know where to spend your money. Invest your efforts in winning over those who post negative comments about you!

The study of politicians recommended by their enemies can be used in many ways. For instance, if you hire Bono, lead singer of the group U2, to advertise luxury cars, you know he will boost sales. Maybe what you have not considered is that if the president of a rival brand drives the car you manufacture, he will help to hike your sales of your brand even more.

Be sure to associate with people who project the image you want to portray. Make a famous personality use the watch you make. If you want to look smart, get together with a progressive writer with leftist tendencies. What you should never forget is the saying "The company you keep says a lot about you."

"If you want to be liked, associate yourself only with those who are likeable."
Jean de la Bruyere

6. PRINCIPLE OF CONSISTENCY
If I say so, I will do so

"Your actions do not let me listen to your words."
Anonymous

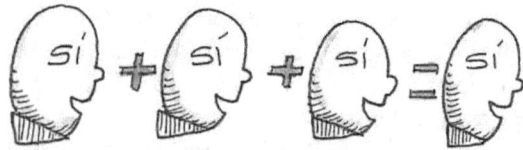

If a claim is recorded or there is a witness, it will tend to be consistent and congruent with what was said in the presence of people who read it or heard it. If you think something is good or bad, you will tend to justify actions according to that pattern.

I have a childhood friend, who on several occasions said to his brother and me: " Blue is my favorite color." Once we grew up, as an adult, he was talking about buying a new car and said he was thinking of the purchase of a red one. His brother and I questioned him by asking "Isn't blue your favorite color?" The day came when he went to the car dealer accompanied by his brother. Upon arrival, his brother exclaimed, "There is the car you like. Hopefully they have it in blue!" Which color do you think he bought?

A toast to Mr. Smith!
Timeshare sales representatives have realized the power of this principle.

Imagine the scenario - you are sitting down at the table in a room, surrounded by twenty people pretending to be interested buyers. More than twenty minutes have gone by, and you start to feel uncomfortable. At this point, you have said "yes" several times. Do you want to have breakfast with us? **"Yes."** Would you like to tour the facilities? **"Yes."** Would you like to have an apartment without paying a high price for it, let us say 80% cheaper? **"Yes."** "Congratulations Mr. Smith! The sales representative gets up and clinks on his glass calling for attention, "Let's make a toast to Mr. Smith, who is now one of our partners!" You stare at everyone in the room, raising their glasses with fake champagne. You express to the sales representative your concerns about your finances: "I have to check my budget." The representative replies "But you just said that you are interested in owning an apartment!"

In this session, the representative has applied several key mentally powerful techniques. You are already his victim. His psychological mechanism forces you to avoid confrontation and, on the other hand, it encourages you to be consistent: you end up signing or leaving by giving excuses that you should not have had to make up.

You have already said "yes"

How does a man who wants to conquer a woman, apply this persuasive principle? In a straightforward and classic fashion, by inviting her out several times. Just like in the example of the timeshare, she also accepts on several occasions. Maybe she is just interested in the places she has been invited to. After going out on multiple occasions, and talking about their interests, hobbies, food, music, and types of men she is drawn to, he is adapting to those characteristics as much as he can. He knows he will never be six-feet-tall nor have blue eyes like Ryan Gosling nor big pecs like Will Smith, but he knows the profile of her ideal man and focuses on those characteristics that are similar to that imaginary ideal.

Agreeing to go out with him is her first "yes." The day after, she gives a second "yes" by accepting to go to a concert. By agreeing to go out to eat sushi, her favorite food, she is giving her third "yes," and watching a movie with her favorite actor (**yes, yes, yes**). Finally, the man kisses her in front of her house.

The man if short, far from looking like Brad Pitt, does not exercise and has not spent a lot of money, but he has already kissed her! Why? Because unconsciously, he has been consistent with what she said about her ideal man. Even if he is not perfect, he is getting closer to what she dreamed of. Repeatedly agreeing has a powerful effect on the mind.

The consistency of government

This principle may affect a whole country. Look at what the ex-secretary of the American Treasure, Bob Rubin, says in his autobiographical work. He states in his book that for the Americans to grant the financial support requested by the Mexican Government at the beginning of fateful 1995, it was necessary that "Mexicans agree to make meaningful changes in their policy."

He also adds: "The president was committed to economic reform. The most important aspect of this reform was interest rates... the Mexican negotiating team in Washington with the IMF had rejected higher interest rates. In his meeting with [President] Zedillo, the IMF trader Larry dealt with this problem after forty-five minutes of polite conversation on all issues related to the bailout. The President thought for a moment and replied: 'For all my career at the Bank of Mexico I wrote articles stating that Mexico should have positive interest rates. Now is not the time to give up that idea".

Shortly after the meeting that Rubin reports, interest rates in Mexico rose to 100%, after having been a few weeks earlier in only 7%. The North American team, according to Rubin, considered that their trip had been "a complete success."

The skills of Summers, the American businessman, made President Ernesto Zedillo consistent. It is such a good example that it is worth re-reading it: "Throughout my career at the Bank of Mexico, I wrote articles stating that Mexico should have positive interest rates. Now is not the time to give up that idea". The president was very consistent and the American very skilled, as Alan Greenspan himself called it. (15)

Are you a pacifist or are you with Obama?

The principle of congruency or consistency in social psychology refers to how people change attitudes when they are exposed to persuasive communication. There are three elements: **P** (recipient), **S** (sender) and the **O** (message itself) (16).

President Barak Obama (S) makes a positive public announcement about the war (O), and a citizen (P) listens to it.

There is a scale to measure the reaction of the recipient, where a +3 is very positive, 0 is neutral and −3 is very negative.

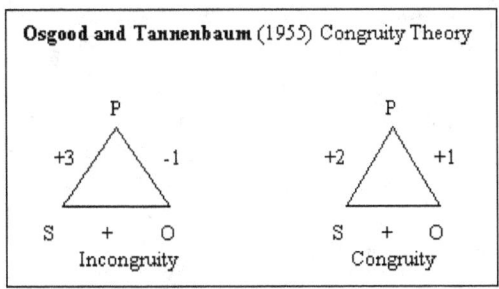

Theory of Congruency
Lack of congruence
Fig. 1

Before the announcement - The first triangle shows how the American citizen liked (+3) Obama (P- S), and he slightly disliked the (-1) war (P - O).

The second triangle shows what happens with the attitudes of the citizen after processing Obama's declaration. This solves the incoherency in his mind, making it consistent! Now the American citizen likes Obama slightly less (+2) and likes the war more (+1). This theory, at this level of revision, suggests that what changes are what has fewer points on the scale. That is, what one likes the most is what will prevail in the face of incongruity.

In this model, there are two main assumptions that happen in the event of a more marked incongruity.

The first is called constant assertion and says that with a high degree of incongruity (Obama speaking in favor regarding a form of discrimination) it is more likely that the person will change his attitude towards the source (Obama), becoming more negative and then changes his opinion about the concept stated in the assertion or message. That is, it is more likely that he will dislike Obama more (although he used to admire him) than to change his mind about discrimination.

The second hypothesis is known as correction of incongruity. It explains that when there is a considerable incongruity between the message and the source (Obama speaking negatively about his own race), it may be that there is no change in attitude and there will only be disbelief and doubts regarding the reliability of the message (manipulation of the media).

Yes, but no... or yes?

A dad who says he loves his son but beats him, is a "yes, but no" that creates internal conflict. "If I love him, why do I beat him? Maybe I do not love him that much?" Dissonance is also very common among consumers who buy something expensive and later experience buyer remorse: "Was it really a good purchase? Why did I spent so much on this purchase if I need to pay for other things?"

Cognitive dissonance refers to the tension or internal disharmony in a system of ideas, beliefs, and emotions that a person perceives when having two conflicting thoughts simultaneously (17). People will do everything possible to reduce disharmony and achieve consonance. Also, will avoid all situations or unfavorable information that may increase conflicting thoughts. Cognitive dissonance is a feeling that arouses disgust and is caused by breaking the law of consistency.

This state of dissonance is very useful in persuasion. "Remedies" offered to justify purchases; balms of tranquility reinforcing the ego: "Sir, by buying this luxury car, you are purchasing security for your children."; "This jewel will be part of an estate for future generations and will never lose its value"; "A percentage of the sales value of this product will be designated to fund a good humanitarian cause." *Voila!* You no longer have dissonance and can be congruent. Ah! What a relief!

Dissonance is always stronger when there is a discrepancy between thoughts and actions, for example, by doing something that embarrasses us. This is how self-justification came about: "I beat my child because I want to educate him"; "I am thrifty and am buying this as an investment." The individual attempts to deal with the "threat" by using justifications.

An example of cognitive dissonance is smoking. Cigarette smoking increases the risk of cancer, which threatens the self-concept of the smoker. Most of us believe we are intelligent and rational, and the idea of doing something foolish and self-destructive causes dissonance. To reduce this uncomfortable tension, smokers tend to make excuses for themselves, like saying "I'm going to die anyway, so it doesn't matter" thus minimizing dissonance. However, it is also true that dissonance can make people stop doing something and change their behavior, such as quitting smoking or drinking alcohol. Understanding what is right for them discourages people from having that dissonance by altering their behavior.

That state is also ideal to persuade further for other types of consumption and activities: "Here in the Eagles Group Alcoholics and Addicts, we show love maturely, come and join us!" "In this Serene World Church, we understand, and will not judge you. Come and start a new life!"

You shall have no other gods before Me

Theodoric VIII, King of the Goths, professed great devotion to the Arian religion. His prime minister and confidant, however, was a Catholic, but to please his master he turned to Arianism. Upon hearing this, Theodoric ordered his execution. When asked for a reason, the monarch replied: "If he could betray his God, I could not trust him" (18).

Human beings perceive consistency as the most basic form of confidence in others and oneself. Trust is the most valuable bio-social survival link in a community. Primitive man judged the acts of others and his own actions regarding consistency between what was said and what was done. Distrust is a lie, and a lie can hurt… literally.

Nobody trusts he who betrays himself. The man loves consistency; we appreciate it because we believe that in "harmony" lies truth and security. We shall call for consistency and dissolve cognitive dissonances. The results will be amazing. You will find a lot to discuss about this conundrum: Despite our search for consistency, we are profoundly inconsistent.

"Inconsistency is the only thing in which men are consistent."
Horace Smith

7. PRINCIPLE OF SCARCITY
It is expensive because it is scarce

"A poor man is not the one who has too little, but the one who craves more."
Seneca

This is the law of supply and demand. When an item is thought to be scarce, people believe that it is worthwhile. If the supply of that item is abundant and anyone can have it, then the item is worth less.

A student asked the wise master the secret of happiness and peace. "Master, I have spent three years without asking anything, as a sign of respect and humility. Yesterday I saw a dead bird falling; it was flying and fell for no reason. I took it as a sign to break my silence and ask about the secret of happiness and peace". The teacher sat meditating for a while and without speaking a word, got up and walked away, only to sink himself slowly in a nearby lake. The teacher never went out of the water. The surprised and sad apprentice understood the last lesson: "Oh master! Now I know the secret of happiness and peace is the here and now, appreciating the scarce air and time left since our brief life can end at any time. How valuable each breath is!"

Good things come in small packages

Imagine a weekend at a department store. You are about to look over an item (could be a tie or a purse), and suddenly, someone else takes one of the two items that were on the counter. There is only one left, and you unwittingly begin to touch it again, you take a closer look and check the price tag. It turns out that it is not cheap and you were not considering buying it. A sales representative tells you: "It is the only one left, they sold out quickly." What are the chances of your buying it? Has this ever happened to you? It often occurs with time restrictions on specials: "Today is the last day of the spring sale," "this fashion sale ends tomorrow," "we are closing on Friday," "these are the only ones left" and many other never-failing clichés that are aimed at creating scarcity.

Let´s recall an old technique of sales applied in furniture stores: a living room set with a "sold" sign is on display. Next to this set is another that has no sign. Which one do you think people will ask for? Exactly... because it cannot be bought. This same technique is used by car dealers, jewelry and clothing stores, and others. Everything can be scarce in some way and thus explains why the forbidden is the most desired: because it is somehow rare.

Homo-economicus

It is important for us to understand an important aspect of the law of supply and demand as described for the very first time by the economist Frederick Taylor; it is simply that the value of something goes up when it is scarce. According to this law, the price of a good lies at the intersection of supply-demand curves. If the price of a good is too low and consumers demand more than what the producers can put on the market, there is a situation of scarcity, and therefore consumers will be willing to pay more *ceteris paribus* (with other conditions remaining the same.)

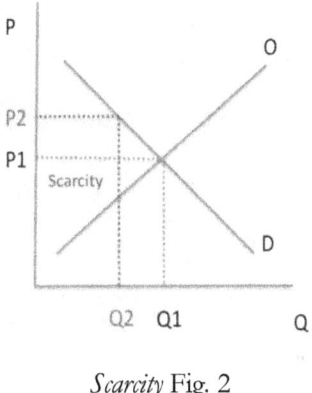

Scarcity Fig. 2

It is amazing to see how we human being act like dogs (it is not my intention to offend dogs). A dog will be jealous if his master pets another dog, and will demand attention and try to remove the hand of his master with the tip of his nose. He is afraid of losing the love and care of his owner and feels threatened. We can also observe this behavior when dogs guard their food or toys with selfishness.

Psychology explains the phenomenon of scarcity through the "Theory of resource conservation." According to this model, people try to retain, protect, and create resources. What is threatening them is their potential or actual loss (19).

People seem to be more concerned about the possibility of losing something than by gaining something of equal value. An example of this is the fact that we pay more attention to text messages that come over our phone than to the person in front of us. Both conversations have the same value, but we prefer to read the text because we are afraid of missing an important message. It is a scarcer form of communication and therefore more valuable.

There is a condition of scarcity that economists call the "Owner-ship effect." When an object forms part of a person's patrimony it immediate increases in value, so we want more for something we own than what we are willing to pay to acquire it. People place a higher value on an object simply because he or she owns it (20).

For some reason, everybody exhibits this behavior of seemingly misleading economic logic. Let us use as an example the watch that you bought years ago for no more than $50. Years go by and then the watch is now a collector's item, and the market value goes up to $500. The principle of scarcity in its variant of the ownership effect adds an affective factor to the mix. You would not like to sell the watch at the current market price, but at a higher price due to the emotional connection.

It seems irrational, but an object acquires an additional value by the mere fact that it belongs to us because of the imaginary projected shortage. Consciously or unconsciously, people think that once they sell the item, it will increase in value because it will become scarcer. Collectors are more practical since they lack that strong attachment and are easily able to exchange items or sell them at prices set by the market.

Few monkeys, lots of money

There is the story of a well-dressed gentleman who visited a small village, stayed in the only hotel in town, and put a full-page notice in the local newspaper. He was looking for monkeys and was willing pay $10 per animal. The peasants, who knew that the forest was full of monkeys, ran out to hunt them.

The man bought, as promised in the advertisement, hundreds of monkeys at the stipulated price. There were very few monkeys left in the forest, and it became harder to hunt them, so the villagers lost interest. Then the man offered $15 per monkey, so the peasants ran back into the forest.

Each time there was fewer monkeys and man raised the offer to $20. The farmers returned to the forest, hunted more of the few remaining monkeys until it was almost impossible to find one.

Now the man was offering $50 for each one. As he had some business to take care of back home, he left his assistant in charge of the monkey business.

The assistant made a new proposal, "Look at this cage full of hundreds of monkeys that my boss bought for his collection. Now that he has left, I am willing to sell them back to you at $30 each, and when my boss comes back, you can sell them to him at $50 each."

The villagers got all their savings and went running back to the assistant, buying all the monkeys that were in the cages. They waited for the return of the gentleman who never came back again. The only thing left for them was a cage full of monkeys they had bought with their lifetime savings (21).

The above story has been repeated time and time again throughout history and in financial sectors. The stock market collapse in 1929 was the result of an analogous situation. Many countries around the world have suffered the terrible consequences of fake expectations of "bubbles" in the stock market.

Why scarcity?
Set Godin gives several reasons for promoting shortage in products or services.

- Scarcity creates fashion. People want something others do not have.
- Taking place in line creates demand. People want what others want, which is why they sometimes spend hours in line to get the newest phones.
- Scarcity also generates word-to-mouth advertising, because people talk about their place in line, the failure of other related products, and make remarks about the positive characteristics of the product they are purchasing.
- Finally, the shortage of a product or service separates true believers who are willing to make a sacrifice. They will more likely be the voice and light in viral marketing. Since

they made an effort to purchase the product or service, they are more apt to talk about it and even feel entitled to do so (22).

Scarce scatology

The law of scarcity goes hand in hand with the perception that a group of people needs it or appreciates it. An old phone made in the 70´s is scarce, but no one considers it valuable. On the other hand, "Fountain" by Marcel Duchamp's is one of his most famous pieces and consisted of a standard urinal. The ceramic urinal was displayed upside down at the Grand Central Palace in New York in 1917 and turned into an artistic success of this period. It is now described by the 500 most influential people in British art as one of the most important art pieces of the 20th century. Therefore, what makes something valuable or not?

Duchamp may have thought that it was just art, but it was also science. Through his work, he demonstrated that any object could be considered a piece of art if placed in an appropriate setting and displayed as such. The scarcity of this work in the context of the time and place where it was exhibited, made it shine and as worthy as gold. That urinal, for mere historical reasons only, is still valuable.

Think about what "museum" wants to exhibit your valuable "urinal." Doing so may make a difference in your life, but remember that you do not have a lot of time: life is short.

"Scarcity is the lack of something, and it is from that scarcity that desire is born. However, the most important thing is not to desire, but wish to desire ".
Dalmiro Sáenz

8. PRINCIPLE OF AUTHORITY
I obey the doctor's instructions

"Authority is the balance between free will and power."
Emanuel Levy

People tend to follow the instructions of someone who is considered to be an authority to unimaginable extremes.

"Authority" refers to the justification and the right to exercise power and opinion. For example, while a crowd has the power to punish a criminal (as in lynching), people who believe in the rule of law assume that only a court has the authority to order a death sentence. Finally, the proper authority justifies the act of killing another human being.

Stanley Milgram (1963), a psychologist at Yale University, conducted one of the most famous studies in psychological obedience. Milgram conducted an experiment focused on compliance and awareness of what is right or just.

He examined the justifications made by the defendants accused of genocide during World War II at the Nuremberg Trials. The argument given by most of the defendants was based on obedience, and almost everyone said that they were only following orders from their supervisors.

Milgram was interested in investigating the extent to which people would obey an instruction even if it meant hurting another human being. The participants were recruited through advertising in newspapers to participate in a study on learning at Yale University. The sample group consisted of 40 males between 20 and 50 years old, and whose occupations ranged from unskilled workers to professionals.

At the beginning of the experiment, each participant was introduced to another participant, who was, in fact, one of Milgram's team members. The participants rolled dice to decide who would be playing the role of "teacher" and who was going to be the "student." However, everything was set up so that the team members always played the "student" role. There was also a "researcher" dressed in a white lab coat (like a doctor), played by an actor.

The student (also an actor) was tied to a chair in another room with electrodes on his body. After studying a list of word pairs that were given to him to memorize, the teacher asked the student to name a word from the pair of multiple-choice answers on the list. The teacher was instructed to administer an electric shock every time the student make a mistake and to increase the level of shock each time he was wrong. There were 30 intervals on the console shock generator, ranging from 15 volts (mild shock) to 450 volts (danger, severe shock).

The student then would (on purpose) gave many wrong answers, and for each of them, the teacher had to give him a shock. When the teacher refused to administer a shock, and turned to the researcher for guidance, he was given a standard instruction consisted of only four possibilities:

1. Please continue
2. The experiment requires you to continue

3. It is absolutely essential for you to continue
4. You have no choice but to continue

Sixty-five percent of the participants (teachers) had to apply the highest level, 450 volts. All participants went to 300 volts (23).

Milgram carried out 18 variations of his study with equivalent results. The conclusion: ordinary people are likely to follow the orders given by an authority, even if they hurt an innocent human being. Milgram (1974) once said: "The legal and philosophic aspects of obedience are of enormous importance, but they say very little about how most people behave in certain situations. I carried out a simple experiment to prove how much pain an ordinary citizen would inflict on another person simply because he was ordered to do so by an experimental scientist. The authority faced the strongest moral concerns when people had to harm others, but even when listening to the cries of the victims, authority prevailed. The extreme willingness of adults to do almost anything upon command by an authority constitutes the principal finding of the study."

Factors Associated with Authority

1. **Status of location** Yale was the perfect location due to the university's prestige.
2. **Personal Responsibility:** when the responsibility is less, obedience is greater. When the researcher had an "assistant," 95% pressed 450 volts.
3. **Legitimacy of authority:** people obey if they recognize the authority as legal or right.
4. **Status of authority:** the actor was called "researcher," and was wearing a lab coat, a symbol of being a scientific expert with high status. When the same actor dressed normally, obedience was almost null. A uniform gives status.
5. **Support from others:** when friends support the opposite order, obedience decreases. Also, if participants see other subjects disobey, they too tend to obey less.

6. ***Proximity of authority:*** it is easier to challenge the figure of authority when we are removed from it. Obedience decreases to 20% when instructions are told over the phone from another room. If the participant is near the authority, obedience increases significantly (24).

I respect your authority only if I am aware of it
The British philosopher and mathematician Bertrand Russell was invited to give a lecture on politics at a club of conservative women.

Because of the leftist speech he gave, the ladies began to throw everything within reach. To avoid worse problems and rescue the philosopher, a guard tried to appease the angry crowd. "Ladies, but he's a great mathematician, a great philosopher!" he insisted without much success. Finally, he shouted: "His brother is a Royal Count!" Calm returned to the room, and Bertrand Russel was safe.

Authority and leadership
Some factors facilitate imposing authority on certain occasions, but do not generate influence or command instantly: authority is context-sensitive.

Inherent authority in a role, when used correctly, should be sufficient to produce some effect on subordinates in a corporate environment, but not to gain their full commitment just because you are the "boss." This requires that the inherent authority has the full support of his subordinates. Be a leader to gain authority.

Some factors involved in leadership are:

1. ***Respect:*** arises from the recognition of each person as unique in the multiple tasks and roles he/she plays.
2. ***Coherence:*** is not to betray principles and ideals; walk the talk.
3. ***Empathy:*** the ability to understand each other's position.

4. **Commitment:** active involvement in the achievement of common goals.

Authority and confidence

According to a study by scientists at Cornell and Washington universities, authority makes people feel taller than they really are (25). In one of the research experiments scientists measured up to 68 people. Then, a third of them was asked to write an essay about a time in their lives when they had exercised authority over others.

Another third of the volunteers was requested to write about a time when they had been in a state of submission. The rest was asked to write about things that happened the day before. After this exercise, all participants were asked to estimate their size in relation to a pole which was adjusted to always be exactly 20 inches taller than their objective heights.

Men and women who had written about a past situation of power tended to point their estimation of height in an exaggerated scale, compared to participants who had written about a situation of submission.

The researchers noted that participants felt taller if they had talked about a previous position of power. In two other experiments with almost 200 volunteers, it was also proven that authority affects our perception of our height. According to the authors of the study, these results suggest that when we are mentally strong, we also tend to overestimate our physical size. The question is: Will the perception of authority influence other facets of our lives?

Always pay attention to whether the person who wears the "white coat" tells you something contrary to what would benefit you, and learn to get into that white coat to order something you need. Being a leader helps.

"I need authority, even if I do not believe in it."
Ernst Jünge

9. PRINCIPLE OF COERCION
If you don´t do it, you´ll pay

"A favor that is asked to be paid back is not a favor, it is blackmail ".
Enalco

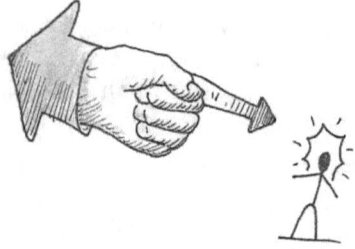

When someone threatens or promises something in return for the other person to do or stop doing something, it conditions by appealing to feelings (positive or negative) knowing that it will affect the behavior. It is about coercion; blackmailing.

Do you know that daily you are blackmailed in several ways without being aware of this? It is done by people who advertise all sorts of products and brands: soup, charitable foundations, and even rock bands. Does it sound strange? Maybe so, but it´s a fact that a lot of persons and organizations manipulate you in a daily basis by emotional coercion.

Imagine that you suddenly hear the hit song that speaks of a lost lover who was cheated and abandoned. It is obvious that you are that lover and your love will continue until the end of time. The song is sad, and you are too. You identify with the song, and it becomes one of your favorites. Thus, singer, producer, record label, lyrics, radio commentator, everyone involved in this production is blackmailing you, without anybody realizing it. This is a massive undercover extortion that kidnaps your feelings.

They appeal to something very intimate that you feel, that you have and share with millions of people. They do this to promote the song, so you buy the album or download it from iTunes. This blackmail technique is also used for movies and many other products. For example, a TV ad that features a Boy Scout who has nostalgic memories in a camping trip: "I love the soup my mother cook." Ready ... blackmail already happened without your noticing it! There is no evident coercion.

Blackmail typically relies on guilt and fear: "I have pictures of you naked with other people, give me money or I will make them public." But the feeling of nostalgia comes from an occult blackmail based on sentimentality. Like the girlfriend that cries about everything, expecting her guy to do what she wants.

Blackmail is most used with the people we love: "You do not love me anymore, do you?" "If you don´t do this, I'm going!" "If you behave well, I'll buy it for you." "If you do not fix your room, you do not go out." We abused the innate compassion of the human being.

Blackmail-ology
There are six fundamental aspects of emotional blackmail (26).

1. **Demand:** in an implicit or explicit way, there is something wanted from another party. "I want to marry you."
2. **Resistance:** the other party does not agree with the demand, "I do not want to marry you, but I do love you, it's just that I am not ready yet."
3. **Pressure:** perceiving resistance, the demanding party puts pressure on with all sorts of questions and powerful

statements. "You always told me you love me. Prove it! If we don't get married, it means that you don't love me".

4. **Threat:** if resistance continues, an ultimatum or threat follows: "If you're not willing to get married, I'm out of here, this relationship is over."

5. **Obedience:** the resisting party yields, out of fear, as a result of the threat; "Ok, let's get married! I honestly love you, and although I don't want to get married, I don't want to lose you".

6. **Reiteration:** once there is an apparent sense of peace, and once the resisting party has given up, blackmail is completed, and roles have been defined. The demanding party knows how to manipulate the other party.

Don't get involved

Not becoming a victim of blackmail is easy if you follow the next steps:

1. **Define your position:** "I do not want to get married yet."

2. **Explain your needs:** "I love you, but I must focus my resources and time on pursuing my master's degree.

3. **Be clear about common agreements, what can be tolerated and what cannot:** "We can think about it in March of next year, but there is no way during the next six months."

4. **Accept or reject:** "If you agree to talk about it later on, great, that will make me very happy, but if not, I will understand."

The duck

A child was visiting his grandparents on their farm. He had been given a slingshot to play in the woods. As much as he practiced, he never managed to hit his target. One night when walking home for dinner, he ran across his grandmother's favorite duck. Impulsively he threw a stone at the animal, and it went directly to its head. The child was frightened and hid the dead animal in a pile of wood. He realized that his sister Mary had seen everything, but she said nothing. Later that day, after lunch, the grandmother said: "Mary, let's wash the dishes." She said, "Grandma, Joseph told me he wanted to help you in the kitchen." Then she whispered to her brother: "Remember the duck?" The boy washed the dishes for an entire year.

When the "principle of blackmail" is applied, several kinds of reactions can be aroused in the other party: an intense desire to help, or fear, or guilt, or shame, or a feeling of emptiness appears.

Superstitious and obedient pigeons

Punishment is implicit in rewards and vice versa. If you do "this" you will get a "reward"; otherwise, you will be "punished" in some way. It scientifically known as conditioned reinforcement, and it can be positive or negative. It works for taming any human or animal. There is a reward if we do a successful somersault, or when a button is pressed. There may also be one or two electric shocks. It is "reward or punishment." Frederic Skinner was the scientist who revolutionized this long-standing and well-known concept.

Classical conditioning

Skinner wrote more than twenty books and about two hundred scientific papers while he was a professor at Harvard. He could send a missile with pigeons trained to peck circles and control it, or could make two pigeons play ping-pong or ride in toy cars, but he was not a circus performer. In fact, it was his scientific background that allowed him to manipulate behavior.

Skinner's thoughts developed an impressive and cruel experiment that is commonly referred to as "superstition among pigeons":

1. Several pigeons are put in an enclosed area.
2. A device is placed that frequently and at brief time intervals, provides them with food.
3. This device is automated to provide food from time to time, and independently of any actions by the pigeons
4. The result is that the birds seem to go crazy and die (27).

Why? The reason is that the pigeons had just repeated exactly what they were doing at the time of receiving the food: circled counter-clockwise, ducked, scratched, wildly flapped its wings, etc. They became "superstitious." The birds think that if they do this, they will get fed, but die instead.

Yes, I am submissive, and so what?

Every day Frank prepares breakfast for his wife in the morning. After combing her hair, he cleans the bedroom and makes the bed. Later he goes to work for many hours and upon returning from his day at work, takes her to dinner or prepares her favorite dish. He washes and irons all the clothes. He seldom visits his family and naturally does not have many friends. He is completely devoted to his wife, who does not work nor moves a finger at home.

Undoubtedly, there are many women in the same situation. Gender is not the determining factor. The question is: How did the partner manage to have an accommodating servant who also seems to be happy with the situation? Answer: conditioning; coercion, blackmail, making angry faces, fights, rage, and all kinds of negative reinforcement, but also implicit is positive reinforcement: "Dear, if you do everything the way I like, I will make your life easier."

"What is the basic principle, the essential, the crucial difference between freedom and slavery? It is the principle of voluntary action against coercion or compulsion".
Ayn Rand

10. PRINCIPLE OF ATTRACTIVENESS
If someone is appealing, I will agree.

"If you want to be president, do not lose any time; get a video and practice during hours how to get better looking on T.V.".
John Anderson

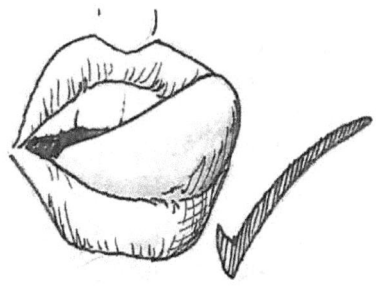

If someone or something is perceived to be attractive or beautiful, there is a greater chance for having agreed to what is being requested.

Our personal image, aesthetics or beauty have always had a positive impact on others. It is easier to attract attention, people, ideas, sex, votes, everything has to do with appearance and beauty. Over 83% of the choices we make are based on what our eyes perceive (28). We live in a world where the appeal of the visual prevails, where images are the only language and become the major consideration. An image is not only worth a thousand words; it is The Word in itself.

Such supremacy of beauty and attractiveness is felt daily. In recruitment and selection, the best potential candidates are not necessarily selected for a job. During these processes, image play a huge role. At workplace, employees who are considered the most attractive receive higher wages, are easily promoted, and even are considered more intelligent. Studies have shown that in primary schools, the "cute" kids get better grades.

A set of circumstances, cultural values, socioeconomic status, age, and country are all factors that affect our perception. However, there are some elements that are becoming universal; values, concepts, and ideas are homogenizing due the Internet and social networks that make it increasingly easier to become familiar with and to recognize the attractiveness of other cultures.

I trust myself when I look good
The attractiveness of an individual goes beyond the visual and the evident. It is a matter of things so subtle as the tone of our voice, our aroma, height, movements, personality, the sound of our laughter, and many other details that make human beings so particular and unique.

Self-confidence is a common universal denominator. We communicate our confidence in the way we walk, talk, and the way we address others. It is the secret of beauty as perceived by others. Being attractive starts by being confident and having respect for ourselves. External beauty reflects your internal beauty, so bear in mind that charm starts inside you.

A survey of 11,000 people carried out by London Guildhall University showed that those who describe themselves as physically attractive earned more money than others who describe themselves as less attractive. The people who have described themselves as less attractive earned, on the average, 13% less than those described as more attractive; also, overweight people earn 5% less.

This may merely be due to self-esteem but what is certain is that the variable "physical appearance" is related to this assertion.

Appealing is beautiful

Even with the variety of parameters and preferences that exist, you can manage to improve your attractiveness. There are certain universal parameters, certain aspects that are useful because they bring us closer to the collective unconscious consideration of our concept of beauty and attractiveness.

The stereotype of physical attractiveness is a concept that psychologists use to refer to the tendency to assume that those who are physically attractive also possess other socially desirable personality traits. People who are happy, sociable, friendly, and successful are also desirable. Society appreciates these traits.

Stereotyping acts as a prophecy. Society also automatically considers attractive those who are valuable and they receive preferential treatment. Studies have corroborated that higher personal income, social skills, and self-confidence are related to attractiveness (29).

What makes an object attractive?

There are few objections to the statement that "beautiful is desirable", but the real question is: What makes something beautiful? The answer is not simple, but it is easier to understand if we apply certain universal considerations when defining an object as beautiful:

1. ***Geometry:*** human tends to prefer geometric figures, especially in what we create. Natural objects are rather fractals in shape, and we appreciate them as well.
2. ***Intrinsic value:*** if something is considered a classic (Ford T) is scarce (diamonds), designed by someone important (a famous artist), iconic (related to an age or period) or has any value *per se*, automatically it is beautiful.
3. ***Golden ratio:*** the number *Phi* (1.618033989) as part of its composition as a ratio. There are many examples:

credit cards, LCD screens, architectural facades, the human body, paintings, etc.

4. **Simplified unit:** having few different geometric shapes that are perceptible. The simplification of materials, parts, features, colors, components, and measures.

5. **Symmetry:** if we divide something and it looks the same or mirrors an image, this is pleasing to the eye.

6. **Expressive or neutral:** neutral gives a subtle expression and therefore minimizes the impact and goes well with any decor. On the other hand, the expressive can be contrasted and enhanced. Both are recognized as good-looking expressions. Anything in between them is perceived as mediocre.

What is attractive in a person?

There is an endless list of studies about what is deemed to be physically attractive. We will describe them pragmatically, which may seem to be a blunt approach, but the length of each consideration forces us to be concise.

Attractive male

Symmetry: symmetrical face and body are preferred.

Body odor: sometimes a subject is judged as of better smell and becomes more attractive (usually the symmetrical persons are considered as having better odor).

Genetics: complementary immune systems are preferred; sometimes perceived by the sense of smell.

Age: they are preferred mature (not old).

Ratio waist/chest: body in "V" (shoulders wider than waist).

Muscles: strong but not too muscular.

Genitals: if large, increases his attractiveness.

Height and posture: taller than women, upright posture.

Hairiness: is preferred on the face and body only in some countries.

Skin color: unimportant, a slight preference for darker tones.

Attractive female

Symmetry: symmetrical face and body are preferred, large, well-defined eyes with space in between, small nose, thin jaw, small ears, and wide forehead.

Age: preference for younger women, depending on the age of the man. Women are considered more beautiful between the ages of 18 and 40.

Bust: symmetrical and firm, larger in the western world.

Buttocks: round and firm.

Body mass: average, not too fat nor too thin.

Ratio waist/chest: smaller waistline than hip with a proportion of approximately of 0.70 (for instance, in Scarlett Johansson her 23 of waist divided between 35 of hip, equals to 0.66).

Height and posture: shorter than the man.

Legs: long legs, 5% longer than the length of the average population is considered more attractive.

Hair: long and shiny.

Movement: gentle swing to her walk.

Skin color: light or dark, well taken care of; reddish tones over yellowish ones.

Eye Color: unimportant.

How to look more attractive?
Men: pin-up shoes, clothing, buttocks, teeth, and cleanliness.

Women: improve posture, clothes, hair, and makeup. Quality underwear enhances natural qualities.

Everything is relative
Although there are verifiable trends and studies on issues considered "universal," nothing is absolute. What is felt to be attractive is culture-dependent and changes according to different aesthetic patterns and trends of the times. Social relationships influence this perception, behavior and even gender differences. The same applies to all objects, the ordinary or vulgar can suddenly become beautiful.

It is also true that the influence of physical attractiveness in social relationships is evident when you consider that the most attractive people have better access to some locations, occupy leadership positions within a group, and may be judged more favorably. The most beautiful objects also sell better and are worth more.

People who look good, have an advantage in being better at persuasion, but one must not use this as the only criterion, which would be dangerous and ultimately ineffective: form and content are equally important.

Think carefully about how to look better and how to make what you do look better too. Your weight or height does not matter as much as what you project. Beauty is the pleasant perception of what causes a positive response in others. It is also a reflection of what people have within themselves at an unconscious level, in their culture, and even in their genetics.

"Some people no matter how old they get never lose their beauty, they merely move it from their faces into their hearts."
Martin Buxbaum

11. PRINCIPLE OF POWER
If you give me power, I will follow.

"Most powerful is he who has himself in his power."
Seneca

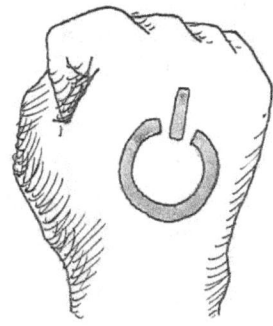

If a person makes you believe that thanks to his/her power you will achieve certain benefits such as: sexual favors; love; political, economic, or spiritual influence; you will follow him/her.

Power is an ambiguous concept that can accommodate all wishes and their likelihood of occurring. It is undefined and based on the aspirations of others. Politicians live to make people think they will have greater purchasing power, making their colleagues believe they will be able to get an advantageous position at the cabinet level. It is the most primal motivation-engine for humankind; the survival of the ego.

Nefarious Power
We follow those who we think can give us something we desire: love, safety, information, or a sense of belonging.

The strategy of nefarious power is the following:

Promise: let others believe that everything will be better.
Submit: punish and limit those who do not deliver what you want.
Broke: destroy rules, institutions, friendships, and values to get what you want.
Unite: Bring together ideas, people, enemies, friends. Build bridges based on interest.
Feign: be prudent about what you say and do. If it is good, be sure it looks as so. If it is bad, make it be perceived as good.
Evidence: have some proof that your actions are in benefit of the others.

Leadership: antithesis of Nefarious Power
The main feature of an innate leader is the strength that comes from his/her ideas and convictions. This strength can´t be pretended.

According to new statistics, four out of ten employees quit because they considered their boss incompetent (30).

In general, managers often confuse leadership with being able to discipline or fire a subordinate. This misconception causes the third part of all workers to view their bosses as ineffective and poorly trained. Increasingly voluntary resignations are related to this social phenomenon.

Recently, the company DDI for talent management introduced the findings of research conducted with 1,279 workers in the US, UK, Australia, Canada, China, Germany, India, and Southeast Asia, to find out what employees think about their bosses. The conclusion was there is much discontent among employees regarding attitudes of their immediate superiors.

For example, 34% of the employees said that they seldom considered their boss effective; 37% of them are unmotivated to give the best of themselves. A lack of communication and empathy may be the main causes of this situation.

Only four out of every ten employees say that their superior does not hurt their self-esteem. While half of these ten felt that they could do a much better job than their boss, only half would want to take his place. This finding points to the outlook for the future supply of leaders. It seems that there is less commitment to such a large responsibility.

According to this research, 49% of employees said their boss had seldom taken them into account to solve work issues that concern them. The study noted that the most common mistakes in the exercise of leadership are not listening, the inability to deal with conflict, favoritism, a lack of information and a lack of consultation with staff.

Moreover, seven out of ten respondents said their boss became upset and did not show a positive attitude when discussing a problem. The nearly 1,300 employees surveyed agreed that a good leader must be able to:

- Properly identify the attitudes of his employees.
- Support them on an ongoing basis and talk to them when there is a decline in their performance.
- Involve the employees in the decision-making process.
- Listen.
- Take time to explain decisions that relate to their job.
- Respect and maintain intact the self-esteem of his subordinates.

The 48 laws of power
The famous book by Robert Greene and Joost Elffers, *"The 48 Laws of Power"* brings together wisdom, several authors, and classic characters such as Sun Tzu, Liddell Hart, Niccolo Machiavelli, Confucius, Napoleon Bonaparte, Julius Cesar, and others.

In the list below, I discuss these laws with phrases in bold letters, to enhance their value by qualifying them, and in some cases, contradict them.

1. Not outshine the master. **A: be assertive.**
2. Never put too much trust in friends, learn how to use enemies. **A: trust your instincts.**
3. Conceal your intentions. **A: have good intentions that can be expressed.**
4. Always say less than is necessary. **A: be prudent.**
5. So much depends on reputation – Guard it with your life. **A: do not die defending your ego.**
6. Court attention at all cost. **A: associate with something positive.**
7. Allow others to work for you, but always take the credit. **A: give credit to those who deserve it, it will be more beneficial for you.**
8. Make people come to you and, if necessary, use bait if necessary. **A: Do not fish sharks.**
9. Win through your actions, never through arguments. **A: if you do not win, explain why you lost.**
10. Infection: avoid the unhappy and unlucky. **A: try to help them without risk for yourself.**
11. Learn to keep people dependent on you. **A: develop independent people who will be loyal to you.**
12. To disarm your victims, use openness and generosity selectively. **A: have more allies than victims.**
13. When you ask for help, do not appeal to peoples' mercy or gratitude, but to their selfishness. **A: be careful that by feeding that ego it does not end up eating you.**
14. Pose as a friend, work as a spy. **A: almost always people can tell when you are not sincere.**
15. Crush your enemy completely. **A: befriend each of your enemies whenever you can.**
16. Use absence to increase respect and honor. **A: when so appropriate.**

17. Keep others in suspended terror: cultivate an air of unpredictability **A: surprise people!**
18. Do not build fortresses to protect yourself. Isolation is dangerous. **A: live together or perish.**
19. Know who you are dealing with. Do not offend the wrong person. **A: do not offend anyone, no matter how unimportant they are.**
20. Do not commit to anyone. **A: commit to those who commit to you.**
21. Play a sucker to catch a sucker – seem dumber than your mark. **A: the art of war is based on deception, but the art of love also works.**
22. Use tactics of capitulation. Transform weakness into power. **A: reemerge from the ashes.**
23. Concentrate your forces. **A: on the weakest point of the other person.**
24. Play the role of the perfect courtesan. **A: do not prostitute yourself.**
25. Re-Create Yourself. **A: keep your mind healthy.**
26. Keep your hands clean. **A: and your head too.**
27. Play on people's need to believe to create a cult-like following. **A: have faith.**
28. Enter action with boldness. **A: between doing and not doing, always do.**
29. Plan all the way to the end. **A: when you cannot, improvise based on genuine intuition.**
30. Make your accomplishments seem effortless. **A: even if there has been no effort, make it seem so.**
31. Check the options. Make others play with the cards you dealt. **A: do not dole out many options.**
32. Play with peoples' fantasies. **A: when you finish the game, be careful not to cause resentment.**
33. Discover each man's thumbscrew. **A: make sure Achilles doesn't realize this.**
34. Act like a king if you want to be treated as such. **A: be a righteous king.**
35. Master the art of timing. **A: practice it!**

36. Scorn things you cannot get. Ignoring them is the best revenge. **A: do not worry about what people will say, that way you will not have to seek revenge.**
37. Create compelling spectacles. **A: and affordable ones.**
38. Think as you like but behave like others. **A: or join forces with those who think and behave like you.**
39. Stir the waters to ensure good fishing. **A: but don't get your sleeves wet.**
40. Despise the free lunch. **A: pay when you must.**
41. Avoid stepping into a great man's shoes. **A: stand on their shoulders to see further away.**
42. Strike the shepherd and the sheep will scatter. **A: sometimes the source of trouble (shepherd) is yourself.**
43. Work on the hearts and minds of others. **A: and with yours as well.**
44. Disarm and infuriate with the mirror effect. **A: when someone does this to you, catch him off guard by not becoming furious.**
45. Preach the need for change, but do not change too much at once. **A: change what you have and can change.**
46. Never appear too perfect. **A: be aware that we are all perfect even if we are wrong.**
47. Do not go past the mark you aimed for; in victory, learn when to stop. **A: do not always try to be at war, seek peace.**
48. Assume formlessness. **A: adapt (31).**

Choose between being Machiavelli or Jesus, characters who could handle power. Note that the two of them were tortured: power always implies a responsibility and a cost. In both cases, the two of them were physically injured, but only one had a transcendental impact. So, before seeking power, find the meaning behind what you do. This will be the best guide to use your power correctly.

"After having power, there is nothing so excelling as knowing how to use it." Jean Paul

12. PRINCIPLE OF INCENTIVE
You can have this if you do this

"War and massive risks also have incentives."
Anonymous

The humans act according to stimuli and will accept whatever they believe is convenient for them to reach their interests.

Social psychology and sociology agree in saying that this principle is decisive in human relationships (marriages, teams at work, dating and in societies). They call it the "social exchange theory" and explain it as a process of exchange negotiated between people in which all human relations are based on the cost-benefit ratio concept. For example, when a person perceives the costs of a ratio to be above the benefits, he will terminate the relationship.

We can say that people respond to stimuli, rewards, and incentives even without realizing it. People are rational and always consider the risks involved in every one of their actions.

An incentive does not refer only to money. Programs of organizational incentives, for example, know that it is not enough to offer financial rewards to employees who reach a certain level of performance or productivity, but rather must have comprehensive programs for employees to feel recognized and appreciated for the adequate execution of their duties.

Rewards must be handled accordingly to individual preferences because what might be attractive to an employee or consumer, will not be so for another. Thus, banks now offer customizable "rewards programs" for their clients: miles, discounts, exclusive programs, etc. They know that not all customers are the same and try to offer tailored programs for each of them.

Incentives not only generate positive emotions, satisfaction, recall or brand positioning; they can result in an emporium as well.

Chewing gum, bubble gum
William Wrigley traveled from Philadelphia to Chicago when he was 29 and only had $32 in his pocket, but great skills as a salesman. His father was a soap manufacturer, so William began selling it under the brand "Wrigley." As an incentive, he gave away baking yeast with the purchase of soap. When the yeast turned out to be more popular than the soap, he switched to the business of making baking yeast. In 1892, William decided to motivate consumers by offering two packs of gum free with each can of baking powder. The special offer was a great success. Once again, the promotional gift was more attractive than the product being marketed, so he started selling chewing gum. If you are not familiar with the brand, it might be worthwhile reading the fine print of chewing gum wrappers to realize how large this emporium is. It stems from the principle of incentives.

The economic logic of life
Some economists have been successful writing books about incentives: Among them are Steven Levitt and Tim Harford. Their approach is quite interesting because it is based on the premise that

humans, and virtually all living beings, are rational. The word "rational" does not mean that human beings are intellectually brilliant, but that we have a logical behavior based on incentives and not so much on feelings or randomness.

Harford has cited several examples of interesting experiments confirming that the "principle of incentive" is the behavior of how living things respond to stimuli causes. We will react positively when something is easy, cheap, or beneficial; and negatively, when it involves more cost. Incentives virtually dominate our lives (32).

Incentives for safe sex and not to commit crimes
There would be a decrease in unprotected sexual practices if it were mandatory for teens to notify their parents about abortions. Tim Harford presents this study - Lick and Tratmann (2005), in which adolescents unconsciously avoid the embarrassment of telling their parents they are pregnant and at risk of contracting AIDS. Similar studies by Steven Levitt (2005) show that those states with earlier and stricter punishment for teenagers dissuade them from committing crimes in their adult years (33).

Tougher penalties = less crime
More shame = less risky sex
Incentive = desired action

Managing rats
In a famous laboratory experiment, rats were given a certain amount of tonic water or root beer for them to administer a "budget". (34). It was proven that the decision to manage consumption of bitter tonic water and delicious root beer depended on the price (number of times the lever was pulled) and salary (the limit of possible lever pulls). Of course, the rats did not know what the amount available was, but they budgeted just by seeking and receiving stimuli. People usually act in the same fashion, even if we are not aware of our administration efforts, costs and rewards.

Loser / Winner

At the Olympic Games in St. Louis, Missouri in 1904, during the marathon, Fred Lorz was the first competitor to cross the finish line and as the winner was rewarded with a laurel wreath placed on his head by Alice Roosevelt, daughter of the sitting U.S. President Theodore Roosevelt. Almost immediately he was disqualified for cheating.

It turns out that halfway through the competition, Lorz began to feel ill, so he decided to get into the car of a police officer who was driving by. He asked the officer to take him to the stadium to pick up his clothes, because of his indisposition.

He traveled in the car the 11 kilometers to the stadium. Once inside, and having recovered, he came out of the car, and as a joke began to run again in the Olympic Stadium, crossing the finish line. The audience was excited, believing he was the rightful winner and he was swept away by the excitement of the events. Once his hoax was discovered, he was stripped of the award.

Fred Lorz was encouraged by shame, pride, and the desired prize, so the following year he won the Boston Marathon, this time without any tricks. Incentives are the natural food of action; look for your own; find those that motivate others and use them. Give me an incentive, and I will move the earth.

"Women... if they inhabited the moon, there would be more astronauts than grains of sand in the sea".
Ricardo Arjona

13. PRINCIPLE OF SUBCONSCIOUS
Guide my dreams

"The subconscious is the history of mankind from the beginning of time."
Carl Gustav Jung

The subconscious (unconscious) mind acts at the same time as the conscious mind, with the difference that people do not realize it. This is the submerged part of the iceberg. He who guides the largely unconscious mind has in his hands the will of the people.

His book was almost ready to be published. He was just missing one minor detail: the title! His editor gave him an ultimatum: "If by tomorrow you do not give me a title worth a million dollars, I will order it to be printed as 'Use Your Noodle to Get More Boodle.'"

The author decided to seek the support of an ally, his subconscious mind; the set of thoughts we are not fully aware of, and that can turn into actions we are unaware of while awake, or our thoughts while we are asleep.

The author was Napoleon Hill. He did go to bed with the firm conviction that he would have the appropriate title the next day and he left to his subconscious thoughts the task of finding it. He woke up the next morning, called his editor and said, "I now have the title of the book, *Think and Grow Rich* (35)." It was a bestseller, the second best-selling book in history after the Bible.

Our subconscious mind always acts at the same time as our conscious mind but without our noticing. It is an alternate mind, a decision maker which is part of us, the secret guide that leads our will, without our will being aware of this.

Every day we encounter situations where this "alternate self" makes decisions; however, it does not make some of the decisions, which are induced.

Eat to miss my class reunion
I make a conscious decision, "I will eat here because I like hamburgers." Subconsciously, what happens is that the predominant orange and yellow colors of the hamburger joint send a message to my senses and make me hungry.

The "M" logo looks like a breast. I used to eat here with my ex-girlfriend and I miss her. All this takes place while I watch a clown smiling, sitting outside the local fast food place. All of this speaks about happiness, and along with the aroma of freshly baked bread, I go back to my childhood and special moments. (Ray Kroc said once: "It´s the name, that glorious name, McDonald´s. You can be anything you want to be, it´s limitless, wide, and open. It sounds like… America. As compared as Kroc… would you eat in a place named Kroc´s?") At the same time, I know that hamburgers make me sick; which will give me the perfect excuse to miss my class reunion! How many things am I thinking without being aware of them!

Internal dialogue

Conscious: "I am a young woman, and I like that man."
Unconscious: "Your lotion reminds me of my dad and how he smoked. He used to look like that when I was little. I find that red shirt really attractive. His eyes widen when he sees me, and there is something hypnotic about the fact that they tell me I am pretty. His pheromones tell me that he is ideal for my type of genetics".

You look familiar

Zajonc and Bornstein's experiments on subliminal exposure were famous for making subconscious mental processes evident. In the first part of the experiment, a group of participants was exposed briefly to images of different faces. In a second interview, they were asked to identify the faces they had seen earlier; but after not being able to recognize them, they were asked to point to the ones they liked the most. They pointed out the same ones they had seen previously. The fact is that you will prefer a face that you have seen before, even if you do not remember it (36).

The next part of the experiment was to very briefly show to the participant's subliminal images (in a film where they were not obvious, but hidden in a frame) along with two people who we will call X and Y. After that session, the subjects, as well as X and Y, were asked to discuss and determine the sex of the author of several poems. Without the volunteers being aware, X and Y would disagree, forcing the participants to mediate. Just as the mere exposure hypothesis had predicted, subjects tended to support the person whose face had been seen unconsciously in the film. Those who saw X in the subliminal film supported X, and the others Y, just because they saw the picture for a few fractions of a second!

Subsequently, Bornstein made a deeper analysis of research on subliminal exposure. His finding was important. It is easier to influence the emotions of people when they are not aware of this.

There is something called "subliminal activation of emotions." (5 milliseconds or 1/200 of a second), where the image of a grumpy o smiling face is displayed very briefly, depending on the emotion you wish to show. This action is masked so that it is not obvious nor remembered, and an image of another object or person is presented. Whether someone likes it or not will depend on the smiling or angry face that was induced subliminally.

How to create a sublime message
1. Choose a message (name, brand or call to action)
2. Turn it into an image or a sound
3. Reduce it to the minimum with respect to other messages
4. Mask or hide it (deception)
5. Design a solid distraction
6. Repeat it
7. Test and improve it

Social psychologist, John Bargh's experiments, showed that the hair length, skin color, sex, height, and other physical characteristics, activate stereotypes that influence the way we interact with others, even if we deny it. In other experiments, it was surprising to find that some people who were asked to form sentences about the elderly moved slower and walked as elders without realizing it while thinking about the task. The same thing happened with the subjects who believed of words related to be a determined or educated person.

For instance, we may treat someone kindly, for instance, because we like (subconsciously) Asians. This will obviously benefit us, but what about those reactions we do not control, like seeing a blond-haired person or a tall one, or any other characteristic associated with an internal prejudice? You will surely see adverse consequences from their reaction once they note this, which in turn can play in your favor or against you.

Self-persuasion

We can use our subconscious to better ourselves, as proposed by Émile Coué de la Châtaigneraie. This prestigious therapist asked people to repeat 20 times for several weeks the following sentence: "Every day, in every way, I'm getting better and better." Achieving this may be the secret of happiness, as proved by many studies conducted with people who practiced this simple discipline.

Another way to persuade us is by using a neuro-linguistic program, which as complicated as it sounds, is straightforward to apply. It is about changing the mental patterns that do not help us for others that will, like a computer program that needs to be replaced or updated.

Imagine that you must interact with someone who is not pleasant or that you are in a scary or uncomfortable situation with him. Think about that person (also applies for groups) and place him on a black and white television screen so you can remember him. Now, literally hallucinate that you can make the following changes in that image:

Visual changes

- Nose, clown clothes, and shoes.
- A pink dress made for a six-year-old girl.
- Broom-like hair, mess with the hair as much as you want.
- Pancho Villa mustache, even if it is a woman.
- Groucho Marx glasses with eyebrows end moustache

Audio changes

- Donald Duck's voice.
- Background music from "The Simpsons."
- Stuttering

Kinesthetic changes

You are now part of that television image and begin to feel how you transform and grow like Hulk: your muscles increase in size, your clothes get torn, and the image of the person gets smaller. The person wobbles comically and breathes heavily. With your large hands, you put this picture of the transformed person in the palm of your hand. This individual image is like a small postcard stamp that you can deal with. Notice how you are no longer afraid of the person or of coming closer to him. You have rid yourself of your self-limiting prejudices.

You are now free and able to practice these exercises; you will taste the power of subliminal persuasion in yourself and others.

"The conscious mind may be compared to a fountain playing in the sun and falling back into the great subterranean pool of subconscious from which it rises."
Sigmund Freud

14. PRINCIPLE OF ANTAGONISM
Join me against him

"Antagonism grows everywhere where life is manifested in the eternal struggle between the individual soul and the social soul."
Yoritomo Tashi

When there is an enemy (real or imaginary) against which to fight, individual wills will join collectively and focus on a common goal. Being against something affects everyone, and therefore is a principle for the survival of the species.

China has believed, since ancestral times, that *Yin Yang* represented good and evil contained in a circle. The *Tao* is the meaning of life; everything moves in this world due to this duality: hot and cold, water and fire, man and woman. This apparent antagonism generates energy. For this same reason, successful people believe it is good to have enemies or rivals.

Even some modern marketers argue that brands should have competition and that it is a mistake to avoid it, given that categories need to become larger and this can only be achieved through opposition. How can a product look "better" if there is no parameter with which to compare it?

When there is antagonism, ideas flow, competition starts, advertising gets nourished. The wind collides with the wings of an airplane to make it fly, gravity and the opposite masses of celestial bodies make our galaxy and our planet move and rotate. This is the universe, antagonistic by nature.

By telling someone "no," we are enforcing his internal desire of a "yes," and the same is true in the opposite sense. This force or principle of opposites seems an impediment rather than a tool to persuade. It is actually a very powerful principle which uses force to get another person to do what you want him to do.

There is no Batman without a Joker

The movie *Unbreakable* starring Bruce Willis and Samuel L. Jackson is a perfect explanation of the need for an antagonistic force. David Dunn (Bruce Willis) discovered the power of being unbreakable and decided to use it to do good. His antagonist, Elijah Price, (Samuel L. Jackson) found this power in Dunn and was relieved since he was exactly the opposite, a person who broke his bones all the time, a mixture of imperfect osteogenesis and bad luck. One was a good character and the other a bad one. Elijah Price understood everything: "Now that we know who you are Dunn, I know who I am. I am not a failure! Everything makes sense now! In a comic, do you know how to tell who the villain is? The exact opposite of the hero, and most times they are friends, just like we are!"

Elijah understood that everything has its opposing force, which sometimes appears to be antagonistic, but always complementary. Where there is no matter, there is no antimatter; where there are no criminals, there is no police; where there is no darkness, there is no light.

Brawny weightlifters

Strong muscles are shaped by resistance, in the same way, political parties and organizations are formed, for instance, the Republican and Democratic Parties, and companies like Apple and IBM. One of the best techniques to persuade people to follow you is by generating opposition. It does not matter if it is just a little bit of resistance, but it is an option, a counterweight, a "no" to a "yes." People sometimes believe that it is part of their purpose and they look for a way to fulfill their purpose in this "boring" world. It is the way they find to give meaning to their lives.

Wilhelm Reich, in his book *The Mass Psychology of Fascism*, explained how the origin of this political movement did not solely arise from economic factors in vogue at that time or the activity of political leaders. But rather from the collective expression of the average citizen, whose primary biological needs had been ruthlessly crushed by an authoritarian and sexually inhibited society. Any form of mysticism organized as an authoritarian government or religion, feed on the desires of the masses, and we shall come to realize their destructive potential (37). The fascists understood this very well, and pure antagonism convinced millions to fight in a cruel and devastating war.

"Oppose and be free" is the cry of an alleged liberator that resonates inside many people, and we all fall into this trap at some point in our lives, in our desire to improve something that we can't define. Was not every new religion born to oppose something else?

Defense of an opposing force

We can already think of ways to persuade through opposition, but we must also be sure how to defend ourselves in case any counterparty wants to use this principle against us. The best way is not to oppose directly, a principle used by the Japanese in Jujitsu and Aikido and psychologists use it in reverse psychology.

In a fight the opponents push, pull, or hit in the opposite direction, using force to harm their adversaries. It is useless to resist because only greater coaction from the opponent will come about. It is better to use inertia or force the opponent like in Judo. In everyday life, if your child says he does not want to go to his swimming lesson or does not want to eat, tell him he does not have to. Pretend that it does not matter, and inertia, their strength, and their need to counteract will lead them to change their minds.

Do not resist

Something similar takes place in business, and there will always be someone who debates just to be annoying. Let him talk, even for a moment, repeat what he says to show your understanding of his point of view. However, do not say anything to the contrary, as this will generate more resistance. At some point, he will concede and say that there may be alternatives or will analyze the issue to try to understand it from your perspective. It is an amazing effect.

Graphically we can equate a bull about to charge with all its strength. If the bullfighter confronts the animal he will perish on its horns; if he lets it pass, he will be safe. This is similar to any confrontation; you can stoically withstand the force of your dissident or stand aside and try to feel a rapport, so the other side will finally agree.

It is in your hands

Almost two thousand years ago, there were two schools in a city, headed by two renowned scholars: Hillel and Shamai. The problem was the two schools were remarkably antagonistic.

One day, Shamai's students thought of a new way of discrediting the other school. Their goal was to humiliate the wise Hillel. Their idea was to catch a butterfly, and one of them had to take it live in his hands to Hillel's house and ask him if the hidden butterfly was dead or alive. If the wise man replied alive, then the boy would squeeze his fist slightly to show that it was dead. If the answer were that the butterfly was dead, the boy would open his hands and let it fly away, proving it was alive.

The plan seemed perfect. They caught a butterfly, and one of Shamai's students took it into his hands, and they went to Hillel's house and knocked on the door. The wise man opened the door, asking "What brings you here?" The students responded: "We want to know how wise you are." Hillel replied, "And how are you going to know this?" "We will ask a question." "Go ahead" he answered. "I have a butterfly in my hands, is it dead or alive?" Hillel looked at them steadily, guessed the trick, and said, "The decision is in your hands" (38).

There is no struggle without an antagonist. Oppose something, and you will earn a place in the minds of people who want to join your cause. You can call it ego dissatisfaction or genuine conviction. Protect yourself from this principle by letting the force go by, and surrender, without effort or resistance that will only fortify your opponent's muscles.

PB: "Why do you always like to take the opposite view?"
RB: "I never take the opposite view."
Playboy magazine interviewing Roberto Bolaño

15. PRINCIPLE OF PRECEDENT
I believe it because it has already happened

> "A precedent embalms a principle."
> Benjamin Disraeli

We believe that something existed or worked in the past will quite possibly happen and work again.

You only need to be certain that there was an event in the past to be able to create new laws and even perpetuate some far - fetched unjustified ideas. The mind-set of "This is how we have always done it" establishes work processes, social behavior, political practices and of course, mistakes. Past practices validate unfair social horrors, such as: "kill the witches," "women should not vote," "other races should not have the same rights," etc.

In our everyday lives, we also see the compelling power of precedents. It is a very simple way to persuade someone and can convince your boss that something works, "An English company did this three years ago, and they were very successful." You can also use precedents to influence your child that something is dangerous, "Don't do that, you saw what happened to your cousin!".

Precedent is law

Common law is primarily based on decisions made in the past. Legal systems place high value on deciding cases according to consistent, principled rules so that similar facts will yield similar and predictable outcomes in the future. In common law, a precedent has the same legal weight as statutory laws (laws and codes) and regulatory laws (regulations of executive agencies). The precedent is law.

Stare decisis is a Latin phrase which translates into "maintain decisions taken" and is used by lawyers to refer to the doctrine according to which sentences are handed down by a court creating binding legal precedents which can be applied in the future. This short phrase comes from a more extensive saying: *Stare decisis et non quieta movere.* It is a general maxim that once a case has been resolved by judicial decision, it constitutes a precedent which cannot be waived unless circumstances change the *statu quo* and give rise to a need for revising the argument (39).

Life principle

Humanity's decisions are largely based on precedent. We lived for hundreds of years believing as an absolute truth what Avicenna stated about medicine, or what Ptolemy said on astronomy. And we lived under the assumption that "this was how it was done" or "this is what was said" and "this has worked plenty of times in the past" and therefore taken as a fact. It is the quest for a comfortable state that leads us to learn and act based on what has happened in the earlier. Knowing that need for comfort is a source of power for the person who wants to use it in his favor.

Thus, children eat certain foods because we were told they are healthy, or we buy a certain model of car because the one we bought five years ago worked beautifully for us. If you are looking for a job, chances are you will be hired depending on your background experience (which is a precedent).

I am Saint Germaine

Saint Germaine is the name of a mystic remembered as an immortal, wise and seductive man who possessed intellectual and psychic powers. According to stories told, one day a foreigner reached the city of Milan and introduced himself as Saint Germaine. He was dressed in expensive clothes, but no one knew him nor did he have any references to be able to be part of the elite social circle. There was a Harvest Festival on the Via Dante. On a sunny afternoon and to breath fresh air, Saint Germaine went for a walk with his black cape lined in purple. It was Sunday, and society people looked askance, but he walked straight on as if none of this were unusual or new. A poor boy approached him, and SG gave him a gold coin. The boy ran with shouting with delight: "It is gold, gold, a miracle!" People turned with a certain morbid curiosity to see what the commotion was about. SG walked on and went to a place where they sold religious figures and asked the seller to come closer. He said something in his ear and seller dashed off. It only took him three minutes to return, panting and sweating, and handed SG a box of fine ebony - "What does it contain?" pondered the elite community. SG reached out, and everyone thought that if the child had been paid a gold coin, a bagful would be for this product, but SG only gave him a letter. The salesman knelt and kissed his hand, "Lord Saint Germaine, you are a saint." SG kept on walking and people no longer concealed their surprise. They completely stopped in their tracks and whispered in the street. Watching as the man walked with a quiet, unassuming expression, carrying the box of ebony.

As he approached the Piazza del Duomo, a beautiful woman accompanied by her mother appeared, looking over silk fabrics. SG approached them, spoke a few words, and handed the box to the daughter. She happily received it, pass it to her servant, and went and hugged this man who apparently was a stranger (very daring for a woman of those times). The woman's mother could not hold back her tears of joy and shouted excitedly: "You are the most wonderful of all human beings on the face of the earth." SG gallantly waved and kept on going. He found a sick person crawling, begging, and exchanged a few words. All the gossips predicted a fabulous altruistic act, but SG took his staff and struck the beggar so violently that he had no choice but to rise from his fake position and run. People whispered: "What an intelligent man, he knew how to detect a phony." The ensuing rumor that started circulating in just a few minutes traveled so fast that it reached the bishop, who was about to celebrate Mass in the Duomo di Milano Cathedral, only a few meters away. The trusted advisor said, "Your Excellency, a wealthy and righteous man, merciful to the poor, gallant with the ladies, and cunning with scoundrels and said to be immortal is approaching." "Don't let him leave, I want to know him!" said the bishop. While SG continued his way, and upon entering the Piazza del Duomo, the cathedral doors opened, the bells tolled and a messenger guided SG to the bishop who waited smiling on the porch to receive this special guest from the Milan elite. People assumed he was truly superhuman and important, and perhaps thought they were privileged to have a saint named Saint Germaine.

True story: the boy who cried "miracle" was his abandoned and unacknowledged son. The box delivered by the seller contained the ashes of the rich and hated husband of the beautiful woman who embraced SG (her lover in Florence), and who had been killed by the seller in exchange for not losing his properties by ruses (in the envelope which SG gave him were his deeds). The beggar was an enemy, a spy who had witnessed the murder, and the saint, of course, was not the original Saint Germaine, but an individual who used his name and his acts to generate unprecedented expectations and become part of the upper echelons of society at that time.

This impostor was eventually imprisoned, tortured, and beheaded: his real precedents were revealed.

"The previous day teaches us about the day to come."
Píndaro

16. PRINCIPLE OF WRITTEN EXPRESSION
For it is written: The Word of God is powerful

"If one abandons the written word, what other means could carry on Buddha's work?"
Gosho Zenshu

What is stated in writing has stronger influence than what is stated without any record.

They asked American writer Saul Bellow how he felt after winning the Nobel Prize for Literature in 1976. His answer: "I do not know; I have not yet written about that."

We attribute great power to what is put down in writing. So, when we go to a store and check prices, we do not dare haggle, because our mind understands that what is in writing is "law," to the contrary of what happens to those products without a price tag, such as at a rummage sale or flea market.

Our mind is used to obeying what down in writing and accepts it without hesitation. If you are walking and find a "Do Not Cross" ribbon cordoning an area, you do not ask why... this just does not happen. If you read in a magazine that a TV star is violent with his wife, you take it for granted. If you read statistics showing the achievements of a company, you probably believe it because it is down in black and white in a newspaper article.

Priests and police

Religions also exert a powerful influence on "the book says" and "it is written that." There are few religions that survive time and customs without a reference book. All influential religions currently have a sacred text. Without a record in writing, there is no divine principle or way for spreading the word.

Police issue traffic tickets based on written laws and regulations. "It is written here: your car must be towed." You will have no recourse but to accept what is in writing. In any given negotiation, if certain agreements are written, even when not looking official, but were taken by the other party, can obligate the parties to comply with a given action or behavior.

In marketing, some say that what distinguishes brands is not the product itself, but the name. The name is what is in the mind of the consumer. Lots of studies about signs, signifiers, and meanings can be summarized in this: names are what the mind uses to distinguish between objects, people, tastes, feelings, and everything that happens in the lives of human beings so he can understand them. Hence the power of the written word, "the name is perpetuated." It is indelible, undeniable. Thus, in a discussion, a person may be right but has little chance of winning against a written statement. Arguments that emerge from written sources, in someone else's eyes, are much more convincing.

Even the use of traditional writing in psychological therapy helps create a context for new discoveries and possibilities for change. After all, as Nobel laureate Mario Vargas Llosa stated: "Writing is the most rational way of exorcising internal demons."

Lawyers: parents of persuasion

Throughout this book, I have presented several results of experiments in social psychology. The truth is that neither psychologists nor marketers have as much historical experience as lawyers on the subject of persuasion. They are the founders of this art and can offer excellent advice. Below is what they have to say about writing:

Written arguments persuade judges

The prestigious lawyer Andrew Goodman says that written persuasion constitutes an essential tool for defeating your opponent without the need for making him talk. Written Persuasion offers a unique opportunity that must not be overlooked (40).

Writing style is a sure influence

First, if you do not write clearly, the audience will not understand the logic of your argument.

Second, writing style affects the reader 's emotions. Well-written prose makes the readers happy; a reader will have to struggle to understand a poorly written document.

Third, writing clearly and eliminating trivial errors or "typos" will increase your credibility.

Good manners

There is nothing that shows goodwill and good moral character better than writing politely. Always refrain from writing that shows contempt, insult, sarcasm, and offensive language.

Avoid some emphatic words

To demonstrate credibility and good character, avoid words like "clearly" and "obviously." These words will weaken your argument rather than strengthening it and will make it appear that you are insulting the intelligence of the one who is judging you. It's like asking someone in a conversation, "Do you understand me?"

Even more important is not to describe a complex concept as "clear and simple," since this will take away from your credibility.

You need more skill and intelligence to underestimate rather than to overestimate. Do not underestimate the person you want to convince, rather minimize your adjectives without weakening your discourse and make implicit accusations avoiding typical overstatements.

For example, do not change "three" for "many"; "dog" for "ferocious beast"; "company officials" for "overpaid employees." Also, avoid the words "very" and "a lot." It seems to be a paradox, but avoiding adjectives, strengthens your writing. Make proper use of metaphors, do not waste them on intensified attacks (41).

"(Not written) words are gone with the wind."
Anonymous

17. PRINCIPLE OF FAITH
Believe in me, and I will give you a purpose

"A good leader is a seller of hope."
Napoleon Bonaparte

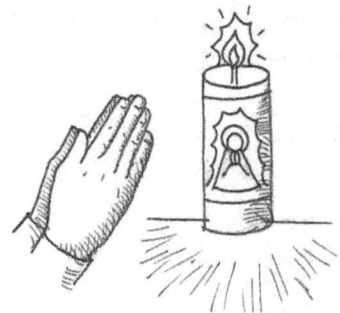

People agree to a lot based merely on faith and will follow if you help them believe in something sublime.

Pope John Paul II received one of the most influential religious leaders of Judaism, the head Rabbi of Israel, Meir Lau, in one of the halls of the Vatican.

The Jewish religious told the pontiff a certain story that took place decades earlier in a European city. Once World War II ended, a Catholic lady went to the church of her hometown to ask the local priest for advice. During the war, she took care of a small Jewish boy who was given to her by his parents before they were sent to a concentration camp. The child's parents had planned a future in the land of Israel for him. The woman was in a predicament and asked the Catholic priest for words of wisdom.

The priest had a prompt and comprehensive response: "We must respect the will of his parents." The boy was sent to the newly born State of Israel, where he was raised and educated. The story was fascinating to Karol Wojtyla, and became even more so when the great Rabbi confessed the identity of that individual: "You, your Eminence, was the Catholic priest, and I was the orphan child."

People do things because they hope their expectations will be fulfilled. Leaders get people to follow them because they expect leaders to be the conduits to achieve their own sublime dream. Pascal's Wager (also known as Pascal 's Gambit) is a posture by the philosopher about the existence of God, which cannot be determined by reason itself. A person should bet on the existence of God and live life accordingly; he has everything to gain and nothing to lose. Just as a child bets his father is always right, so the figure goes on degrading God to father, from father to leader, chief to leader. In all these figures faith can exist and become the energy that drives people to act by their beliefs.

Aspects of faith

In all collaborative human activity, there is a mystique: an underlying belief that is not so obvious. This belief may be elevated to faith when it meets certain conditions:

Knowledge

Faith begins with knowledge of what should be believed. For example, some people know that the gospel of Christ refers to his death, burial, and resurrection, or that the Koran was recited to Muhammad as God's message to humankind, or that Steve Jobs (through a comparison in the world of business) changed the world with Apple. People know these claims and becoming familiar with them is the first step; however, they may know of them, but without fully believing, until they get assertion.

Assertion

Knowledge is not enough. The person must also believe that the object of faith is real. To reach this level of faith, people must not only know what the Gospel, the Koran, or the mission of Apple is (knowledge) but believe it to be true. This is referred to as assertion, but is not enough to provoke a change in the world. To do this, trust is needed.

Trust

Trust refers to a personal commitment and is an object of faith. You can know and believe, but this still is not faith until there is trust.

Say you are visiting someone's home and are about to sit down. You look around and see that there is indeed a chair. This is knowledge. Second, you know the word and the concept of chair and realize that you are willing to accept the offer. You know the chair will hold you. This is assertion. Finally, you walk to the chair and sit down on it. That is trust (42). You are now ready to prove that you have faith.

Proof

Faith is tested; fasting, tithing, building an ark, working for days without sleep. There will be tests that must be passed. Only by *doing* does faith turn into reality.

Live happily

According to Sonya Lyubomirsky, author of *The How of Happiness*, a manual with a scientific basis to cultivate the conditions that can help us achieve happiness, there is a growing number of studies that suggest that religious people are happier, healthier and bounce back from trauma faster than those who are not (43).

It has been scientifically proven that the motivational power of faith, whether this is a placebo effect or a metaphysical manifestation of practice, is necessary. Some agnostics and atheists think faith is not for them, but every time I hear someone say, "I do not believe in any of that, God does not exist", I note that the person releases the need for faith in some ideology such as socialism, or some messianic figure such as Donald Trump.

The best manifestations of faith are seen in people who say they "don't believe in anything". Very frequently they are truly fanatics of something. Some even say that baseball, football, or soccer is their religion! Others carry out their office work religiously, even with rites included. The most highly evolved claim to have faith in themselves, or in humanity and "Superman" as Nietzsche called it. The most malicious may have faith in racial superiority, as the Nazis did, or that they are the chosen people to be the police of the world through a manifest destiny.

Faith is necessary for human beings and has many manifestations. This principle of persuasion is one the most powerful of all and those who know how to control it can dominate the world.

How faith comes about?
Answering this question may seem difficult, but it is not. It is a process and as such has a long gestation. It is easy to define how it comes about, but it's hard to carry out. Nuclear fission is the splitting of a heavy nucleus so that atomic bombs can work. How easy, now do it!

The elements that lead to faith are the following:

Brief transcendental notion
"Save your soul." "Get your freedom." "Change the world." "Stop the abuse." Humans want to transcend and minimize pain. We do not want to die or suffer. The idea should be more grandiose than the world itself. It must seem impossible.

Mystical source
Jesus, Job, Mohammed, Moses, Hitler, Gandhi, Buddha, and heroes from each country are possible channels for communicating

transcendental ideas. The idea itself is not planted in the subconscious; you must have a mental picture to call upon, a type of character who walks in the valleys of our hidden desires. Saying "mystical" does not necessarily refer to the supernatural or superstitious, but can be as rational as socialism, and the leading ideologist became an enlightened saint (Marx) or preserved as sacred relics by his/her evangelists (Lenin).

The media

Communication is important: messages must be divulged by some media in a form of text, image, or speech. At the beginning of time, messages were transmitted orally, but today this can come about in a variety of ways. Churches have diversified the way they spread their message; entrepreneurs and activists have ventured into the unimaginable. Anything goes as long as it is consistent with a transcendental idea: televised masses, testimonies of miracles, mass speeches using statistics of miraculous results.

There is a brand of mangosteen juice that promises to cure virtually every disease. You can even find people with strong scientific background who work at this pyramid scheme company and believe blindly in what they sell and consume.

What is this all about? It may be the power of the so-called "blind faith," or for skeptics, a more tangible aspect such as brain chemistry. Nor should we forget the placebo effect, which occurs when the patient's faith in a medication cures him, although it may be nothing more than a sugar-coated pill. Either way, many members of the scientific community have become convinced as time goes on spirituality can be compatible with science (43).

Since time immemorial, believers and mystics of all religions and spiritual practices have claimed that faith is a vital element of human well-being, including health. Now, new scientific studies agree with those that argue that in many cases faith can move mountains, at least in the field of health. On the other hand, it is important to clarify that all defenders of the power of faith point out that it is not in any way a substitute for medical care, but rather an additional element and can go hand in hand with proper treatment, which can help achieve good health. In other words, faith is a powerful ally of medicine (43).

Spiritual people are happier, enjoy better mental health, cope better with stress, have more satisfying marriages, use fewer drugs and alcohol, are healthier and live longer than those who are not spiritual, according to K.I. Pargament in the *Journal of Clinical Psychology* (44). The divine can be replaced by mangosteen juice or a mission to save the world and whales. What underlies is the desire to believe in something.

A study conducted at the University of Texas that took over 17 years, found that people who do not attend religious services have a higher risk of dying within a period of eight years, unlike those who attend once a week (43). Some people go to the stadium and live truly religious experiences with physical manifestations identical to those of the mystics. Some worship "holy" politicians who give hope for a change in life, while others take a product that offers the hope of eternal youth.

Sonya Lyubomirsky, a social psychologist, has conducted several studies explaining that participation in religious activities decreases crime, delinquency, and marital conflict. The person who belongs to a religious organization feels part of a community that provides mutual support. It promotes peace of mind and helps fight stress, the great enemy of health. The same thing happens in Alcoholics Anonymous, where its founders Dr. Bob and Bill W., succeeded in creating a supportive environment, which is identical to a religion without a given God. Having faith pays off; making people have faith pays off even more.

"Faith is taking the first step even when you don't see the whole stair-case. "
Martin Luther King, Jr.

18. PRINCIPLE OF METAPHOR
If I say heart, understand love

"Eroticism and poetry: the first is a metaphor for sexuality, the second an erotization of language."
Octavio Paz

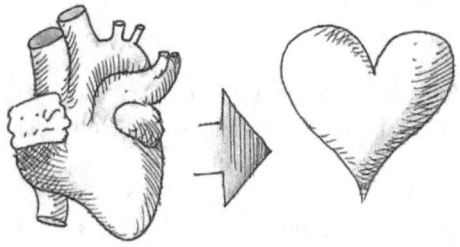

The reality is harsh and cruel; an indirect concept (metaphor, simile, analogy) is much easier to assimilate.

A ninety-year-old man goes to the doctor for a routine check-up. The doctor asks: "How are you feeling?" The old man answers: "I am better than ever! My girlfriend is 18, pregnant, and will have a son". The doctor thinks for a moment and then tells the following story:

"A hunter who never missed a single hunting season left his home in a hurry, but took an umbrella instead of grabbing his rifle. When he reached the woods, he found a giant bear. The hunter raised his umbrella, aimed at the animal, and shot. Do you know what happened?"

—I do not know, the man answers.

—Well, the bear dropped dead before him.

—Impossible, exclaims the old man, —someone else must have shot.

—Of course, that is exactly the point!

Beast or virus

Imagine that your city is not as safe as it used to be. Robberies are on the rise, and homicide rates have nearly doubled over the last three years. What can city officials do about it? Should they hire more police to round up criminals and lock them into a growing network of prisons, or design programs that promise more opportunities in reviewing economic aspects and identifying underperforming schools?

Your answer and the reasoning behind it may depend on the metaphor used to describe the problem according to new research by psychologists at Stanford. Ideas can be shaken up by a single word (45).

Paul Thibodeau and Lera Boroditsky have shown that people are likely to support an increase in the police force and the arrest of offenders if a crime is described as a "beast" that takes advantage of a community, but if people are told that crime is a "virus" that can infect the city, people are more likely to treat the problem through social reform (46).

The findings of both researchers try to explain how subtle cues and common figures of speech can frame approaches to problems. "Some estimates suggest that one in twenty - five words we say are a metaphor" explained Thibodeau, lead author of the study. "But we did not know to what extent these metaphors can influence people."

"We cannot talk about any complex situation, such as crime, without the use of metaphors" commented Boroditsky, an assistant professor of psychology. "Metaphors are not just used as flowery language, but they shape our conversation about things we are trying to explain and understand. They are of consequence for the determination of what is to be decided, the right way to approach and solve problems."

In five experiments, test subjects were asked to read short paragraphs and answer questions about the rising rates of crime in the fictional city of Addison. Researchers assessed the responses from participants regarding how the crime was described, whether as "beast" or as a "virus."

They found that the solutions differed depending on the way the metaphor was presented. In the study, 71% of the participants called for more police reinforcement when they read: "Crime is a beast ravaging the city of Addison." The number dropped to 54% among participants who read the sentence with another metaphor: "Crime is a virus ravaging the city of Addison."

The reports accompanying these sentences contain hard data. Some alarming statistics viewed the problem from a "rational" point of view and mentioned that there were 10,000 more crimes in Addison in 2007 than in 2004 and that the number of murders had risen from 330 to more than 500 during the same period.

All 485 participants in this study were asked to point out what they thought was the most influential part of the report, and only 15% identified metaphors. "People like to think objectively and make decisions based on numbers", Boroditsky stated. "They want to believe they are logical, but they are actually jostled about by metaphors."

You can find ways of communicating your message and the right set of analogies and metaphors that lead people to a favorable or unfavorable conclusion, depending on your approach.

Color, taste, smell, and shape of a metaphor
To know with some degree of precision what metaphor is right for our persuasive goal, we must understand that words have color, taste, smell, and shape. To understand their characteristics there is no better recipe than imagination and to ask ourselves:

What color is the word beast?
It is red or brown.

What does it taste like?
Meat.
How does it smell?
Like an animal.
What shape does it have?
A monster with sharp teeth.
What color is the word virus?
Pale yellow.
What does it taste like?
Like medicine.
How does it smell?
Like cheese or a sick person
What shape does it have?
Scattered in many small points.

With this preliminary analysis of words applied to the example of criminals, it is not surprising that for a "beast" the use of the police force comes to mind, and a call to improve the social network when using the word "virus."

Convincing stories: the metaphor in a tale
It would be impractical to bring up a complex sociological study that proves that telling a story influences an audience more than the use of slides, statistics, and hard data. The entire entertainment industry is made up of stories and music containing metaphoric representations, stories, similes, and analogies that convince us to pay a good sum of money to their creators and producers. This industry is as old as humankind itself. These stories are told by actors who not only entertain us but also through religions that moralize us a society.

What a story must contain
If anyone knows about the art of storytelling, it is Peter Guber, chairman of Mandalay Entertainment. His business is to tell stories. Throughout his career, he has produced some of the best-known films: *Rain Man, Flash dance, Batman, The Color Purple* and

much more. He has also directed Sony Pictures, PolyGram, and Columbia Pictures.

Guber says he tells stories every day, but he has discovered throughout his lifetime that the component that makes a story compelling is the MAGIC according to its acronym.

M = Motivation
Give it your all and be consistent: "If you want someone to do something, you must be consistent, your feet, your heart, your wallet and your tongue have to move in the same direction. When people see something going in another direction, you will not look authentic. Authenticity should stand out".

A = Audience
Think and feel like those who will listen, "Will they connect to you emotionally? Will the encoded information have an impact? Will it be remembered as an emotional experience? Can it be processed?".

G = Goal
We must know what we want: "Goals are very important and we need to bear them in mind."

I = Interaction
Let others participate; it is their experience, not ours. "Frank Sinatra was a beast, a tough guy, but every time he took the stage he chose a woman and started singing for her, and then, in the third act of the show, he would take her and make her sing with him."

C = Contents
The material for stories can come from anywhere: "From your own experience, observations, stories, artifacts, metaphors or analogies, stories; collect them and incorporate them into your corporate leadership practices."

When we tell our friends where to eat or which movie to see, we are transmitting our emotional experiences to them. When you tell stories or use metaphors, we aware that it is better to be the emotional conduit for communication. Always remember to be authentic, it is vital for convincing people.

"In life, everything is a metaphor."
Haruki Murakami

19. PRINCIPLE OF THE UNEXPECTED
What a pleasant surprise, I was not expecting it!

"Irregularity, in other words the unexpected, the surprising, the astonishing, are essential to and characteristic of beauty."
Charles Baudelaire

What is unexpected may be charming and convincing.

In one of his notebooks, Chekhov recorded this anecdote: "A man, in Monte Carlo, goes to the casino, wins a million dollars, goes home and commits suicide."

A tale always tells two stories (47), and surprise is an element of both.

While it is true that there are people who do not like surprises (especially pranks); the truth is that we all like to be surprised, at a restaurant, at the movies, with a joke... There is a definition of laughter that says: "Spasms caused by an unexpected event that is just as ridiculous as surprising." Some surprises make you laugh, and what is more pleasant than laughter? If you cook, surprise your guest with a dish which was not expected but is a favorite. If you own a store or business, give an extra special touch to your customers. If you provide any service, exceed expectations, surprise people, and observe the power it generates. It is so persuasive that people will end up paying more just because they have been surprised. The opposite also works: in war, the well-known " element of surprise" may destroy the moral of the enemy, and with a small army you can beat one five times larger. Even thieves use this element most of the time, and "persuade" their victims to give them money without resorting to strength.

Guide a mind drift to an unknown place, and it will be defenseless against the wishes of the wow-factor maker.

Flanking

The most successful flanking movements are those who are totally unanticipated. The greater the surprise, the longer it takes leaders to react and recover. Surprise also tends to demoralize the opponent. Unfortunately, many times flanking attacks are minimized in effectiveness with "evidence" and excess research that allows the rival to discover the strategy.

Surprise is better than significant experience

American sisters Laura and Kate Mulley handle surprise very well. Neither of them studied fashion nor design. Both attended the University of California at Berkley. Kate studied art history and Laura, literature. Their first foray into fashion was dissecting a Chanel dress, which allowed them to learn how a piece of clothing is put together.

In 2005 they presented their first collection under their own name, Rodarte, at *New York Fashion Week*, where they won the patronage of fashion buyers from stores like Barneys, Bergdorf and Goodman, Neiman Marcus and Nordstrom.

In 2009, only four years after presenting their first collection, they received an award recognition as the Designers of the Year by the *Council of Fashion Designers of America. In addition to this, the Art's Costume Institute of the Metropolitan Museum* acquired one of their dresses as part of their permanent collections.

In the same year, the retail chain Target approached them to collaborate with their designers for a collection that sold out a few days after being released. Recently, they created part of the costumes for the film *Black Swan* and received several nominations in 2011 (48). Rodarte owes much of its success to the element of surprise: What happens when someone who is outside the normal box, designs something completely new? What happens when a "non-expert" proposes something completely novel?

What is not expected and is nice works wonderfully to influence others.

You got all my attention

The physiological response of surprise stems from shock. The primary function of a surprise or startle response is to interrupt an ongoing action and redirect attention to a potentially significant new event. There is an automatic redirection of focus to new stimuli and, for a moment, this causes tension in the muscles, especially the neck, and enhances attention. Studies show that the answer to loud noise, is very fast. A full startle reflex occurs in less than two-tenths of a second (49).

Imagine the ancestral man, this semi-beast whose fear of lightning, animal noises, strong pungent aromas, and flavors, enabled him to survive and instantly discern the good from the bad. That sense prevails not only as a key sensor of survival but of coexistence. Humans pay full attention to something that surprises them on the Internet, radio, or in conversation.

Women know the art of subtle surprise, the balance between what is striking and decent. Publicists shout or whisper, depending on the situation, to draw the attention of the audience. The seller becomes a magician to surprise with low prices or any other trick to impress his prospective audience. The dance of surprise tries to get to us oversaturated with information in a visually polluted world. Not everything that is strong or strident stands out; the relaxed and beautiful also can surprise us.

What surprises, sells

In his book *The Purple Cow*, Seth Godin, decrypts precisely how the surprise factor influences marketing. What would you do if you saw a purple cow? Certainly, you would love it!

1. Differentiate your customers. Look for the group that is most profitable. Investigate which group is more likely to influence other customers. Find ways to develop, advertise or reward. Ignore the rest and take care of customers that if you could, you would choose.

2. If you could choose a market niche that has thus far been neglected and choose your own, what would it be? Why not launch another product to compete with your own?

3. Form two teams: the inventors and the ones who will benefit from the invention. Put them in separate buildings. Hold a formal celebration when a moving a product from one group to another. Then celebrate and rotate people from one group to the other.

4. Do you have the e-mails of 20% of those customers who love what you do? If not, start the list. If you do, what can you offer them that is really special?

5. Being outstanding necessarily means making big investments. It may be the way you answer the phone, launch a new brand, or get a better price. Get into the habit of thinking outside your comfort zone whenever you have a chance. This is the best way of finding out what works and what does not.

6. Explore the limits. What if you are the cheapest, the fastest, the slowest, the hottest, the coldest, the easiest, the most efficient, the strongest, the most hated; the imitator, the stranger, the most difficult, the oldest, the newest? If there is a limit, you should test it out.

7. Think small. A vestige of "television-itis" is the need to think about the masses. "If it is not what everyone likes, then it is not worth the effort." That mentality is obsolete. Think of the smallest imaginable market and describe a product that overwhelms them and will be extraordinary for this niche. This is your starting point.

8. Find things that typically are not done in your industry or sector. For instance, JetBlue Airways almost instituted a dress code for passengers. The company is still toying with the idea of giving a free airline ticket to the best-dressed person on the plane. A plastic surgeon can offer gift certificates. A book publisher could sell a book only for a limited time. A farm supply store, Stew Leonard, took strawberries from the small green plastic containers and allowed consumers to choose the ones they wanted to buy. Sales doubled.

9. Ask, "Why not?" Not everything we do has a good reason to be. Almost everything we do is the result of fear or inertia or the historical lack of someone asking, "Why not?"

10. What about if you simply tell the truth inside your company and to your customers? (50).

"I do not find myself where I look. I find myself by surprise when I least expect it".
Baron of Montesquieu

20. PRINCIPLE OF PRAISE
You are so smart!

"The problem with most of us is that we would rather be spoiled by praise than saved by criticism."
Norman Vincent Peale

We are all vulnerable to flattery; it is difficult to resist.

At the fall of the President of Colombia, General Rafael Reyes (1904-1909), Dr. José Vicente Concha, defined flattery and treachery as follows: "To appreciate the behavior of any public figure, we must consider the atmosphere in which he lives, the air that surrounds him. General Reyes, for ignoble reasons, was surrounded by a cloud of mendacious flattery, a constellation of lies and deceit, many hands covered his ears, and he was blindfolded with many bandages, and yes, he was blind, deaf, and drunk by blarney and stepped down falling to the bottom of an abyss. The "blind guides" that led him there, left feigning shock. Scandalized they started shouting insults against their past idol".

We are all vulnerable to praise. It is practically inevitable not to succumb to this force. Although flattery is contemptible, sincere recognition usually generates a lot of attraction for the person praising us, leading to several studies that show the power of praise.

Get on board

There are many ways to become part of a board of directors of a company, and many of them are related to our ability and skills; however, there are others who know how to sell themselves through chicanery.

A recent study by the Kellogg School of Management, with a long title called *"Stealthy Footsteps to the Boardroom: Executives' Backgrounds, Sophisticated Interpersonal Influence Behavior and Board Appointments"* shows that executives frequently and successfully used subtle but sophisticated techniques of flattery to achieve a position on a board of directors of a Company.

Jest Ithai Stern and Westphal named seven effective tactics used by executives when pursuing a position on the board. They were based on research on interpersonal attraction that included interviews with 42 CEOs of large industrial and service-providing companies.

Stern states: "Past research shows the effects of what happens when corporate leaders make use of flattery and persuasion tactics. However, our study is the first one to look at the effectiveness of specific ways to increase the chances of getting a position on the boards of other organizations, as well as what kind of executives are more likely to use these tactics effectively".

The seven ways to get on a board of directors mentioned in the study are:

1. Disguise praise as if advice is needed. Ask a question seeking advice to flatter the other person. For example: "How did you manage to close that deal so successfully?

2. Deliberate or discuss before agreeing. The employee discusses a point of view before agreeing immediately with the manager's opinion. For example: "At first, I did

not understand your point of view but now I see it, and it makes sense. You have convinced me".

3. Speak well of the supervisor to his/her coworkers. Praise the supervisor to coworkers, in hopes that your words will eventually reach him/her.

4. Frame a compliment as something that can be uncomfortable. Make a positive comment on his/her management, warning that your opinion might be embarrassing. For example, "I do not want to embarrass you, but your presentation was really top-notch, better than most I've seen."

5. Show agreement with values before accepting an opinion, or express values similar to those behind their managerial moral. For example, "I share your point of view. I have always thought that we should increase the salary of the people at the bottom of the ladder".

6. Agree with the points of view the manager has expressed to a third party. Secretly find out some of the views of the manager through his contacts and then express those views in a conversation with him/her.

7. Refer to social affiliations that you have in common with management before daring to agree with his opinions. Mention to the manager any affiliation, such as a religious organization or political party that you have in common. For example, "I watched the debate last night, and candidate X presented some excellent points."

According to the study, managers who have been involved in politics, law, or sales, as well as those who belong to a high socio-economic class, are much more likely to use sophisticated techniques of flattery, than those who have not been involved in this type of activities. The authors note that this proclivity is consistent with the fact that there are fewer senior managers with experience in engineering, finance, or accounting, compared to those with experience in politics, law or sales.

They warn us to be careful with these techniques: "To enter the select circle of the corporate elite, a person dares not be too obvious. Being very open with intentions can be interpreted as a manipulative or political action. The more disguised flattery is, the more sophisticated the approach will be, resulting in more effective results" (51).

Luxury eulogy
Ultra-luxurious brands teach their employees how to sell items in times of crisis. Using praise is the main strategy, for example, it is a rule to flatter the watch of the prospective customer even if it is a rival brand.

JeanMarie Brücker advises sellers to say "value" instead of "price" and selling "romance" instead of "products". It is called the macaroon technique, a word that comes from the French dessert called "macaron" which is stacked: "Sir, this watch (or any luxury item) comes from our best workshop and has a value of $ 12,000. If you buy it, your children will surely enjoy it for many generations." Two romantic attributes are coupled with the concept of value in the middle. Luxury becomes emotion.

Part of the macaroon technique is to place the customer's watch on a tray, next to two new and magnificent watches. This is a subtle way to compare what he already has against what he might have (Principle of Contrast).

Shoppers' remorse plays a key role in the drop-in sales, so experts advice retailers to recommend customers a "gift of apology" for the partner who was absent during the purchase. Another tip is to distract the partners (if present) by offering another item in a separate department. The reason for doing this is not to sell, but to keep the partner busy and distant. The objective is to avoid one of the partners getting bored and asking to leave the store.

In casinos is frequent practice to flatter men, distract their wives, and try to keep them in there as long as possible, so they will likely spend more money. Praise is an important part of an organization orchestrated to sell (52).

Adulation alone is not useful

A study by Florida State University, shows sales pitches create distrustful customers. Is this contrary to the Principle of Praise?

The work done jointly with Darren Dahl of the British Columbia University and Kelley Main of the University of Cork, was published in the *Journal of Consumer Psychology*. This study seeks to determine whether the mechanism by which a consumer decides to trust the salesman or not is the result of a deliberate or automatic process. The researchers conducted three experiments in which 102 buyers participated by purchasing sunglasses: 37 men and 65 women.

In the first experiment, the employees praised the customer before the purchase. In the second, the employees did so after the sale.

In both cases they used phrases like:
"These glasses are amazing", "I think they look good on you", "You look great."

In the third experiment, the seller kindly spoke with the buyer but used no praise.

After buying the sunglasses, participants completed a survey regarding how much they trusted the sales representative. The results were very clear. Even when flattery comes after the sale is made, when it is no longer necessary, shoppers did not trust the sales person.

Research shows that participants distrusted the words of the seller, even though it was obvious that the compliment had no impact on the sales. According to the study, suspicions by the consumer are typical of a society that is crammed with advertising campaigns and premade speeches. People react defensively when they perceive an attempt to manipulate them (53).

It should be noted that sales were not affected negatively, but this experiment is important to have a clear notion of praise's scope. How does praising works if it is perceived as an attempt to manipulate? It is important to be honest, but this is not enough, something else is needed.

If she is beautiful, say she is smart

If you meet a beautiful person, do you think that just by complimenting his/her beauty that is enough to persuade or seduce that individual? Surely not.

Does this mean that praise does not work? On the contrary, praise works and works well, but should be used wisely. Lord Chesterfield understood it perfectly: "An undoubted, uncontested, conscious beauty, is of all women, the least sensible of flattery upon that head; she knows that it is her due, and is therefore obliged to nobody for giving it her. She must be flattered upon her understanding (being intelligent or sensitive); which, though she may possibly not doubt of herself, yet she suspects that men may distrust."

In other words, flattery does work but aimed at the most vulnerable aspect.

Kung fu attitude

Alejandro Sanchez, a prestigious *Kung Fu* master, grades the *attitude* that the student shows in an exercise or form. We can better understand attitude, as referred to martial arts, by watching *Karate Kid*, Mr. Han (Jakie Chan) instructing his young pupil Dre Parker to have right attitude when taking and hanging up his jacket. It seems simple and even annoying to Dre, but it makes all the difference at the end of the film when defeating his rival.

This is the "intent." Speaking of language, there is something here that cannot easily be conveyed in writing. A friend usually says "silly" to me when I say something funny that makes her laugh. That word "silly" does not offend me because she laughs and says it with affection. A compliment acts in the same way; if said with an attitude that conveys fear or hypocrisy; this will be perceived and received in a conscious and unconscious way by the end user.

Counterintuitive flattering

Do you think the following statements are useful for flattering a beautiful woman?

"Your hands are so large, they look like a man's", "Your perfume smells funny, like plastic", you have an eye booger", "I had never seen a woman with dandruff."

Yes, believe it or not that kind of statements help and they are called "negatives" or "negs". It seems counterintuitive to say these words, but if applied in the right context and in small doses, they can help to seduce a person. It is the fishermen's technique: bait, hook, pull, drop, and eventually pull out.

Let's go back to the example of flattery selling luxury watches recommended by Jean-Marie Brücker. Immediately after the seller flattered the watch, she asked the prospective customer to leave his/her old watch between two new, expensive, and shiny ones. It is a form of negative reinforcement, the equivalent of "having an eye booger" that helps to seduce someone in times of crisis to spend $10,000 or even more in a watch.

> *"Do not go against what is rightful to get the praise of others."*
> Lao-tse

21. PRINCIPLE OF SOCIAL ACCEPTANCE
All those people must be right

"1.3 Billion Chinese cannot be wrong about our Thursday jokes."
Overheardinnewyork.com

The more people think or do something in common, the more that influences others to believe it is right or acceptable.

How many times have we seen a crowd outside a trendy club or bar and thought it had to be a very nice place? It is obvious that the bouncer has a basic job: make people wait outside and appear to be selective. In more popular places, we can observe an almost identical effect: when we believe the food from a booth in a food market must be the best around because there is a huge line waiting their turn to order.

Acting as "sheep" is merely a mechanism of anthropological adaptation which is very necessary for the survival of the species, hence its power. It is hard not to follow this principle because it is part of our social structure.

Social proof or acceptance is the mother of all science and technique. From immemorial times on humans have observed what others eat, the plants they use to heal, and the places where they take refuge. The same observation is made today in market research in laboratories and engineering projects. Let's say dear reader that you go on a safari tour and find two bushes with delicious looking berries. Three native people are eating from a blue type, but no one is eating from another bush full of red berries. Which one would choose to eat? It is simple to understand the principle from this perspective, but it is not evident in other aspects of our daily lives. Although this is as necessary as it has always been to survive in our modern jungle.

Women choosing clothes and men
There will be exceptional cases, but usually "the grass is greener on the other side of the fence" or, in other words, "the dress she wants is the same one I want" or "why are there so many women in front of that window display?". Of course, socioeconomic levels partially determine consumer preferences, but behind these preferences there is an ancestral background of selection of food and clothing.

Anthropologists believe that women were once responsible for selecting the optimal seeds for planting and consumption. As well as of choosing the best fur, clothing fibers and materials. What used to be simply a matter of survival, today is social survival. The selection of clothes is based on social acceptance. No, my dear female readers, I know you are unique and not carried away by others. We know you are *avantgarde* and your sense of *mode* (fashion) is exclusive, but "mode" in mathematical terms is defined as the number that appears most often in a set. For instance: the mode in the group {7, 3, 9, 7, 7, 5, 9, 3, 7} is 7 because it is the most repeated number. Hence a purple blouse is fashionable, or the brand of your favorite designer, or a certain hairstyle, but these "ins" are nothing more than a number that is repeated most often in a set thanks to social acceptance.

This principle is so important that it can be encompassed in the phrase: "When in Rome do as the Romans do." Imagine you are invited to have dinner with the Queen of England and you ignore one of the protocols, like eating before the host starts, using the fish knife to spread butter, speaking loudly while she is giving a speech, scratching your buttocks, or not following social etiquette by dressing in a brown suit with a mismatched tie. This behavior would not only be the cause of immediate embarrassment but would also be a good reason for never inviting you again, unless you are very important. Would not it be easier to see what others are doing and imitate them? You do not have to assist to a finishing school in Switzerland; you understand this innately just watching around.

People evaluate situations based on the people surrounding them. The clearest example is a man who is accompanied by attractive women. In the argot of seduction, women who serve as "bait", so others will believe that individually is worthy, are called "pivots" (so effective is the strategy that it even has a name in lingo!) He might be an unattractive man, but if he is accompanied by several beauties, other women are forced to turn and look at him. Consciously or unconsciously they think, "This guy must have something going for him!" There is no need for further hesitation, this fact alone is enough to classify him as an alpha male. It is called preselection, is as old as humankind, and has a counterpart. If one night a man is rejected by many women, others barely will give him a chance. So, if you are of the idea that you should speak only to the woman you like, change your strategy because she will not consider you a desired juicy fruit.

Lopsided employers

It may sound irrational, and indeed it is, but it has been proven that a person who has not worked for a long time, is seen as someone who might be troubled, inexperienced or lacking skills. The recruiter will not be objective but look for defects or flaws even though the candidate may be ideal for the position. Bias is greater and dominates over the person's real qualifications.

On the other hand, it is a common belief that those employees who have been managers at recognized organizations have exceptional skills and attributes. Potential employers' perception significantly raises the level of salary that can be offered to them and narrows the search for the best profile for the position. Virtues are enhanced, and flaws are overlooked. The halo effect again seizes the mind over the candidate's qualifications. A person may be described as "quiet" based on these criteria, and can be regarded as "timid" if the mindset is negative, or "thoughtful" if it is positive; "arrogant" if he has not found work or "with personality" if he has had several proposals.

Politicians understand only too well the power of social acceptance. People who attend their speeches are always welcome because they add value. Credibility is achieved largely by the masses who support them. The work of politicians is to achieve credibility rather than effectiveness.

Credibility = Relative number of people who approve something + Perceived evidence (although not true) + Recommendation of an authority.

Trendy music
Several studies have shown that there is an explanation for the success of a product: social influence. When people know that others are playing certain songs, reading certain books, or going to certain movies, they are prone to make the same choices. It produces a chain reaction that leads to and ensures success.

The journal *Science* recently published an article in which the results of a study that has revealed the mystery of the success of certain musical themes. It seemed unpredictable, but researchers have discovered at least one of the most determining factors.

According to this piece of research, people select a particular song, book or movie, if they believe the product is liked others, so it starts a is a chain reaction.

The authors of this study state, therefore, that success tends to grow because of this effect: the more people listen to a song, the more people will like that particular piece of music. A total of 14,341 people participated in a research study on a web page for teens, which actually was an artificial music market.

They were asked to listen to songs and then rank them on a scale of 1 to 5. Then participants could download the files and the songs. Researchers offered a choice of 48 subjects who were not famous taken from another page, an online space where groups can create their own pages to place them songs for anyone who wants to download them.

Some songs were more popular than others, but the groups of people did not always choose the same songs. Also, the songs chosen by all participants, varied in position on the charts, depending on each group of respondents.

While this study shows that social influence is a determining factor in how we act and that therefore, the songs reflect that their becoming popular or unpopular depends in part on the factor of how individuals influence each other. It is also true that it is difficult to predict which song will be the most successful due to social influence, and the more people involved, the more unpredictable it becomes.

It was shown that the quality of the songs influences the following predictions:

- The best songs are almost never unpopular.
- The worst rarely are successful.
- The selections to the others somehow affect individual decisions (54).

The karate sheep

Master Daiki was meditating in his garden while his students practiced karate in the *dojo*. His weakest student, Amida, was watching him from the ground, sweating while one of his classmates applied a painful wrench to his left arm. The teacher looked like he was in a dream world, Amida imagined the peace felt by Master Daiki while sitting in that beautiful garden and that allowed him to escape his painful reality. He was as usual, relentless with his own physical weakness. Master Daiki seemed to ignore Amida and more than once his teammates beat him abusively, taking advantage of their stronger bodies and the fact that the teacher said nothing.

That day, while Amida was laying on the floor, Master Daiku rose from the position of meditation, screaming a powerful and deadly word from the bottom of his stomach, while a group of royal horses escorted by soldiers were grazing in the master's garden.

A battle started. The powerful bare-handed punches of the teacher hit the horses one by one, while they fell to the ground lifeless. Students who saw this shouted furiously and ran to help their *sensei*. Three strong imperial soldiers tried to defend themselves but were badly beaten by the karate students. The young Amida did not react; he remained sitting down inside the *dojo*.

When the encounter ended, the teacher returned to his place of meditation quietly and without comment. The surprised students still exalted ran to him, saying "Master, they stained your honor! We did what we could to help, but you say nothing!" Daiku opened his eyes and replied: "That was the last lesson I can teach you. I have selected my successor." Embarrassed the most advanced and strong student said: "Is it me, *sensei*?" Master Daiku showed a sly smile and said, "It is Amida."

The enraged students replied: "But he's weak, for more than 15 years he has lost every battle, all of his bones have been broken and he has only a few teeth left." Daiku closed his eyes and said, "Amida is wrought iron, the steel of a sword I've been honing and polishing, waiting patiently for this day. You all are sheep instead; weak followers of the flock. Dismissed".

Master Daiku sat in the same position for hours, even when the emperor's soldiers returned to slaughter him without defending himself, his expression was one of peace and happiness. Young Amida founded a new school of karate that exists to this day and has won most world tournaments. This is a school where meditation and peace reign over thoughtless reactions. Their motto is: "We are steel, not sheep."

Beware of following the herd. Better make a few follow your proposal, then realize how social acceptance works like a magnet that attracts more and more credibility and admiration as your group grows.

"People are like those fish that follow each other since they have better chances for surviving by staying as a group... then larger fishes benefit by eating them together as a group."
Dr. D

22. PRINCIPLE OF SIMPLICITY
I like you because
I understand you

"KISS: Keep it Simple, Stupid."
U.S. Army

What is stated in an uncomplicated way will be pleasant and more influential.

In this age of information overload, it seems impossible for something complex to work without being confusing at first. If the goal is to create a cloud of smoke, perfect... but if the aim is to persuade, sell, seduce, or just communicate, then complexity is the enemy.

Leonardo da Vinci said that "simplicity was the ultimate sophistication". Note that the most famous painting of all times, is the portrait of a simply dressed woman, smiling. It is not a pointillist work or a baroque and complicated scene, yet it took Leonardo a lifetime to create this master piece, which he considered permanently unfinished but still simple.

Winston Churchill words are filled with wisdom: "If I have to give a two-hour speech, I prepare it in only ten minutes. If it is a ten-minute speech, then it takes me two hours". Those close to him knew it would take him six to eight hours to prepare and rehearse for a 40-minute speech. Churchill drew the focus of his speech to a single topic, concluding it with a call to action. His notes often included marginal notes with stage directions, such as "pause," to allow time for the audience to assimilate the ideas presented and experiment the emotions.

Simple does not necessarily mean easy. Note the sales of Apple devices. The first iPod was released and was revolutionary; just one button. How simple! Imagine the investment of time and ingenuity backing up that simple design.

Stephen Hawking is simple
Let's see what the most recognized living scientist in the world say about describing the complexity of the universe.

A model is satisfactory if:
1. It is elegant.
2. It contains few arbitrary or adjustable elements.
3. It is consistent with existing observations and provides an explanation for them.
4. It makes detailed predictions about future observations allowing us to refute or distort the model if they are not confirmed.

Note how beautifully a great concrete mind like Stephen Hawking's operates, so simply. The first and perhaps the key point is the model should be elegant. In his words: "Elegance, for example, is not something that is easily measured, but is highly regarded among scientists because the laws of nature signify to compress a certain amount of particular cases into a simple formula" (55).

Be smart and do not complicate things. Remember that the most successful ads are those that contain few words. The most effective salespeople are those who do not use big words or technicalities in their language. The most aesthetic paintings, the most admirable architecture, and the most powerful formulas ($E=mc^2$) are simple.

Guidelines for successful simplicity
1. Remove. Subtract the unnecessary and the obvious.
2. Add. Just add what is meaningful.
3. Organize. Catalogue, separate the differences, combine similarities.
4. Passion. Pour out your emotions and enthusiasm.
5. Context. Context is as important as the main idea.
6. Time. Under promise and over deliver. Exceed expectations.

Write in a complicated way to be regarded as stupid
There is a misconception that using fancy words when writing will make you look brilliant, but it is just the opposite. In a study in which some text is amended to see how readers judged the intelligence of the author, there was found that as the text became more complicated readers gave a lower score to the intelligence of the author (56).

Difficult names are dangerous
Studies found that participants considered a food additive called "Hnegripitrom" more dangerous than "Magnalroxate". If you try saying out loud both names you will realize that although the second is not a beautiful or understandable noun, at least you can pronounce, unlike the first.

The same effect was found in a fictional amusement park. A game called "Chunta" was thought to be much safer than the relatively dangerously sounding "Vaiveahtoishi" (57).

Buy stocks with pronounceable names
A study suggests a way to increase profits in the stock market. Researchers wondered whether companies with pronounceable codes on instant information services like ticker stock quotes (such

as Google, which is written GOOG), would benefit from the effect of the fluidity with which they are pronounced and thus become more profitable in the market.

They tested this idea with real market data, controlling this industrial sector and the possibility that the most profitable companies might have simpler names. After analyzing data, findings show there is a 10% higher profit on those shares with pronounceable tickers (58).

Knowing this, then STIWSB, FTSE, GMXRPR maybe should shorten their name to TOM, LIK and KIS.

Fluent reading, secure purchase

Another experiment compared consumer's perception of some electric appliances by showing them a written list of features using an easy to read font against another font that was harder to read. Those products that used an easy to read font doubled the number of people willing to buy the product (59).

Simple explanation

An adult Viking was teaching his son the art of building ships. It was not customary to do something more complicated than tradition dictated, but they were determined to build the most beautiful and toughest of all Viking ships.

One day the chief of the tribe came to check the construction and strongly reprimanded the father. So, in no time, a group of huge bearded men destroyed the boat. The son crying asked his father what went wrong. The father replied seriously: "It's simple son, the chief's ship was not as good as ours." The boy took a deep breath and stopped crying.

Always think like Einstein: "You have not really understood something unless you can explain it to your grandmother". If it simple enough, this venerable lady and anyone else will think you are smart and persuasive.

"Nothing is simpler than greatness; in fact, to be simple is to be great".
Ralph Waldo Emerson

23. PRINCIPLE OF I AM
We are all one

"I am who I am".
(Ex 3,13-14)

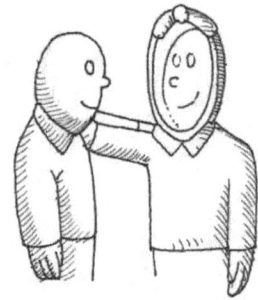

We all share the same spirit and we are all one. If we remember this truth, we will recognize ourselves in each other and will not need any other persuasion principle.

The "Chi" and "Tao" of the Chinese, the "Ki" of the Japanese, the "Force" in *Star Wars*, the "spirit" of the West, the "Om" of the Hindus, the "Attempt" of the Nahuatl Indians, the "I Am"... all of them refer to the same. They refer to be essential, to the piece of God we all have inside us.

Some skeptical individuals may think this idea can be superstitious or lacks a scientific basis, which is why it was left to the last chapter. I am not trying to convince anyone that we all have an essential being, and that it is not the mind but the supra-consciousness what is above all consciousness. What I am trying to convey is that we are all connected. It will be explained to whoever wanted to use it.

Synchronicity

By watching a bank of synchronized fish or a flock of ducks in perfect formation, we can realize that everything in the universe is coordinated by something invisible. How can we explain that certain animals eat a certain type of plant and then the plant develops defenses and deception to prevent being eaten? In turn those animals are eaten by others who deceive with a camouflage that is the same color as the plants around them. Does it not denote a moderating and organizational intelligence?

Eat and being eaten is a perfect circle of power and defense. Who orchestrates this infinite symphony? Chance? Maybe, but even if chance did in an arrhythmic, chaotic dance, this would eventually have rhythm and beat. Even if it was a matter of chance, there must be necessarily a unifying force to coordinate these movements and similarities between living and nonliving things in the bittersweet world we observe today. Rocks almost have the same elements we do, but they do not breath. Someone or something must direct that orchestra of reality. This is the fifth element, the "I Am."

If this law is applied, none of the others are needed because it is the realization of understanding that we are all one. It is "the perfect balance"; some call it the "win-win situation." Even if you are skeptical, you will agree that it is ideal to establish a deep understanding between two persons: If I want to sell you something and you do not want it, do not buy it! But if what I want to sell to is useful to you, do not become defensive, be open to reach the best agreement possible. You will most likely let me help you if you know my intentions to help you come from the heart and what I do is harmless.

Conscious will

We can prove scientifically through neuro-linguistic programming and hypnosis exercises that we can influence an individual who is in an "altered" state of mind. It is not an esoteric or metaphysical subject, it is just something that is proven to happen. That same (but enhanced) effect can be applied with the law of the *I Am*. The principle is very simple; it is to think that "I am in myself and in the other person". We may never know how it works; if it is because unconsciously we transmit information through body language, or by way of hormones or by electromagnetic waves generated by the brain, or thanks to induction by verbal language. Maybe they all form part or none of them do. This is not relevant; the fact is that it works and can be tested.

John Maxwell Taylor, in his book *"The Power of I Am"* explains eight steps to achieve this:

1. ***Disposition to do the job (conscious will).*** Refers to the willingness to do it and to practice. Just as in the same way we develop any skill, we need consistency and discipline. We must focus the mind, body, and emotions on having the intent.
2. ***Self-awareness.*** Your name does not define you, and it does not allude to your identity. I am not Alexander, Rebecca, or John. You are an outside observer of yourself, imagine this. Right now, see yourself sitting reading this book. Notice your breathing, discover details previously you had not discovered. It is not to about "floating" but a subtle shift away from ourselves.
3. ***Focus on the body.*** We believe everything is in our heads, everyone around thinks so as well. When we talk we squeeze our brains in search of the information we think we need. Our body is forgotten and we become talking heads, but the power is in our body, let your mind see your body and remember it.
4. ***Perception and sensation.*** Be aware of your legs, arms and breathing when you talk to someone, practice a sport, play tennis, or write a book, and observe the difference in your performance and the quality of your communication skills.
5. ***Not identified and not react.*** With the same self-awareness described in point 2, learn to observe when you

have a self-limiting thought; or when your internal ego communicates negatively about someone, something or even yourself. Watch it as though you were outside your body and realize that this is not you. Do not criticize yourself because you feel anger, jealousy, envy or hate. Be aware that your *ego* is doing the talking and understand that ego is not your true you. The same applies to your reactions. Do not get offended by something said to you, understand your reactions, and analyze them as an external witness. This will save you a lot of energy and change the dynamics of the internal and external dialogue that your *ego* has.

6. **Seeing eye to eye.** Our eyes are the windows to the soul. If you are right-handed your right eye may show your personality (most commonly) and your left eye may be the window to your *essential being*. If you are left handed, it may be the opposite. That´s a practical approach, but the important thing is to notice the most easy-to-read and kind eye; that is for sure your *essential being* eye (doesn´t matter if you are left or right handed). We want to recognize and be recognized for our essential part, we all have this in common. To achieve this, you need to look casually and set your eyes on the *essential eye* of the person you are talking to. For instance, if you are *essential eye* is in the left, look with it at the *essential being eye* of the person in front (his left eye, for example).

7. **Divide your attention.** Do not get yourself lost in others, do not pay 100% attention to anyone or anything. Always be aware of yourself.

By leaving the illusion of our self-centeredness, we can help people around us to leave theirs. It is easier to sell or buy in this state of essential understanding.

" One by one, we are all mortal, together we are eternal".
Francisco de Quevedo

Bibliography and references

1. **Poeta, El Gato.** El Gato Poeta. [En línea] abril de 2008.
http://el-gato-poeta.blogspot.mx/2008_04_01archive.html.
2. **Garin Guzman, Loreto y Zukerfeld, Federico.**
Reciprocidad. [En línea] abril de 2008.
http://www.cceba.org.ar/CatalogoSala_Nov09.pdf.
3. *Tidd, Kathi L., and Joan S. Lockard. 1978. "Monetary Significance of the Affiliative Smile: A Case for Reciprocal Altruism.".* **Tidd, Kathi L. y Lockard , Joan S.** 1978, Bulletin of the Psychonomic Society.
4. **Cialdini, Robert B.** *Influence: The Psychology of Persuasion.* New York, NY : Quill/William Morrow, 1993.
5. *Is Equality Passé?: Homo reciprocans and the future of egalitarian politics.* . **Bowles , Samuel y Gintis , Herbert.** 1998, Boston Review.
6. **Voltaire.** Diccionario filosófico de Voltaire. [En línea] 1901.
http://www.filosofia.org/enc/vol/e03095.htm.
7. **Dalí, Salvador.** Fragmento de las "Confesiones Inconfesables" . [En línea] 2003.
8. **Ciphra.** *Estudios de mercado de empresas anónimas.* 2011.
9. **Coleman, Daniel.** La práctica de la inteligencia emocional. [En línea] 1998.
http://webs.uvigo.es/pmayobre/master/textos/evangelina_garcia/practica_inte_emocional.pdf.
10. **Pacheco, Ana Belén.** Crítica de Destellos de genio. [En línea] 2009. http://www.muchocine.net/criticas/9756/Destellos-de-genio.
11. **Board, The British Library.** Management and Business Studies Portal. [En línea]
http://www.mbsportal.bl.uk/taster/subjareas/busmanhist/mgmtthinkers/mayo.aspx.
12. **Rosenthal y Jacobson.** Lecture Elaboration: Rosenthal's Work on Expectancy Effects. [En línea] 1963.
http://psych.wisc.edu/braun/281/Intelligence/LabellingEffects.

htm.

13. **Elliott, Jane.** http://www.janeelliott.com/. [En línea] 2012.

14. **López, Alfredo.** Diez curiosas anécdotas de famosos pintores. [En línea] 2011. http://blogs.20minutos.es/.

15. **Salinas de Gortari, Carlos.** Milenio.com. *Ni neoliberalismo ni populismo: democracia republicana.* [En línea] 02 de 2010. http://www.milenio.com/cdb/doc/impreso/8724955?quicktabs _1=0.

16. **Osgood y Tannenbaum.** Communication Institute for Online Scholarship. [En línea] 1955. http://www.cios.org/encyclopedia/persuasion/Ccongruity_theo ry_3osgood.htm.

17. **Festinger, León.** [En línea] 1957. 156.35.33.98/reunido/index.php/PST/article/download/7155/ 7019.

18. **Alfred.** El Anecdotario de Alfred. [En línea] 2012. http://anecdotas.com.es/category/politicos/.

19. **Hobfoll.** [En línea] 2001. http://www.monografias.com/trabajos83/psicologia-positiva-organizacional/psicologia-positiva-organizacional2.shtml.

20. **Harford, Tim.** *La lógica oculta de la vida.* s.l. : Grupo Planeta, 2008.

21. **Garrigasait, Marc.** [En línea] 2008. http://investorsconundrum.com/2008/05/27/un-ejemplo-para-entender-la-bolsa-los-monos-y-los-campesinos/.

22. **Godin, Seth.** Seth Godin´s Blog. [En línea] 2008. http://sethgodin.typepad.com/seths_blog/2008/07/scarcity.ht ml.

23. *Behavioral study of obedience.* **Milgram, Stanley.** 1963, Journal of Abnormal and Social Psychology.

24. **McLeod, S. A.** Milgram Experiment. [En línea] 2007. http://www.simplypsychology.org/milgram.html.

25. *Living Large: The Powerful Overestimate Their Own Height.* **Duquid, Michelle M. y Goncalo, Jack A.** 2011, http://digitalcommons.ilr.cornell.edu/articles/456/.

26. **Forward, Susan.** *Chantaje Emocional.* s.l. : Diana, 2006.

27. *'Superstition' in the pigeon.* **Skinner, Burrhus Frederic.** 2, s.l. :

Journal of Experimental Psychology, 1948, Vol. 38.

28. **Gordoa, Víctor.** *El poder de la imagen pública.* México, D.F. : Debolsillo, 2007.

29. *Does Being Attractive Always Help? Positive and Negative Effects of Attractiveness on Social Decision Making.* **University of Applied Management, Erding, Germany.** 2006, Journal of Experimental Social Psychology, págs. 46, 1151-1154.

30. **DDI.** *Lessons for leaders from the people who matter.* 2011.

31. **Elffers, Joost y Greene, Robert.** *Las 48 leyes del poder.* s.l. : Atlántida, 2010.

32. **Harford, Tim.** *The Logic of Life: The Rational Economics of an Irrational World.* s.l. : Random House Trade Paperbacks, 2009.

33. **Levitt, Steven.** *Freakonomics.* s.l. : William Morrow Paperbacks, 2009.

34. *Experimental Studies of Consumer Demand Behavior: Towards a Technology of Making the Slutsky-Hicks Theory Technologically Applicable to Individual Behavior.* **Batallio, Raymond C. y Kagel, John H.** s.l. : Advances in Consumer Research, 1975, Vol. 2.

35. **Campos , Vicente.** http://vicentecampos.com/. [En línea] 22 de 12 de 2011. http://vicentecampos.com/un-aliado-que-trabaje-mientras-duermes/.

36. *Mere exposure: A gate to the subliminal.* **Zajonc, R.B.** 2011, Current Directions in Psychological Science.

37. **Reich, Wilhelm.** http://michaeljgoodnight.com. [En línea] 2013. http://michaeljgoodnight.com/_Memes%20Books/Chesed-Gevurah/Wilhelm%20Reich%20-%20The%20Mass%20Psychology%20of%20Fascism%20-%203rd%20Edition.pdf.

38. **Aguiló, Alfonso.** www.fluvium.org. [En línea] 2013. http://www.fluvium.org/textos/etica/eti557.htm.

39. www.lectlaw.com. [En línea] 2013. www.lectlaw.com.

40. **Goodman, Andrew.** *Influencing the Judicial Mind: Effective Written Advocacy.* s.l. : XPL Publishing, 2006.

41. **Simpson, Troy.** Persuading Judges in Writing: Tips for Lawyers (And how technology can help). [En línea] 2007. http://www.llrx.com/features/persuadingjudgesinwriting.htm.

42. **Reagan, David.** Learn the Bible. [En línea] 2013.

http://www.learnthebible.org.
43. *The many methods of religious coping: Development and initial validation of the RCOPE.* **Kenneth, I. Pargament.** 4, s.l. : Journal of Clinical Psychology, 2000, Vol. 56.
44. **Hernandez, G.B.** Vanidades. [En línea] 2013. http://www2.esmas.com/editorial-televisa/vanidades/salud/061553/function.date.
45. **Fleming, Chase.** Stanford study shows how metaphors shape the debate about crime fighting. [En línea] 2011. http://www.communicationstudies.com/stanford-study-shows-how-metaphors-shape-the-debate-about-crime-fighting.
46. **Thibodeau, Paul y Boroditsky, Lera.** Natural Language Metaphors Covertly Influence Reasoning. [En línea] 2013. http://www.plosone.org/article/info%3Adoi%2F10.1371%2Fjo urnal.pone.0052961#pone.0052961-Schn2.
47. **Piglia, Ricardo.** Formas breves. [En línea] 1986. http://fba.unlp.edu.ar/apreciacion/wp-content/uploads/2011/05/Formas-Breves-Piglia.pdf.
48. **Elle.** http://www.quien.com/. [En línea] 2011. http://www.quien.com/espectaculos/2011/03/22/laura-y-kate-mulleavy-el-factor-sorpresa.
49. **Kalat, James W.** *Biological Psychology.* Belmont, Calif.: Wadsworth : Cengage Learning, 2009. págs. pp. 357–358.
50. **Godin, Seth.** In Praise of the Purple Cow. [En línea] 2003. http://www.fastcompany.com/46049/praise-purple-cow.
51. **Mays, Aaron.** www.kellogg.northwestern.edu. [En línea] 2010. http://www.kellogg.northwestern.edu/News_Articles/2010/itha i-stern.aspx.
52. **Binkely, Christina.** WSJ. [En línea] 2009. http://online.wsj.com/article/SB100014240529702035173045743 04322707126380.html.
53. **Ray, Barry.** business.fsu.edu. [En línea] 2013. https://business.fsu.edu/press/darke.cfm.
54. *Experimental Study of Inequality and Unpredictability in an Artificial Cultural Market.* **Watts, Duncan, Salganik, Matthew J. y Sheridan Dodds, peter.** 2006, Science.

55. *El gran diseño.* **Hawking, Stephen y Mlodinow, Leonard.**
2010.
56. *Consequences of erudite vernacular utilized irrespective of necessity: problems with using long words needlessly.* **Oppenheimer, Daniel M.**
2005, Applied Cognitive Psychology.

57. *If It's Difficult to Pronounce, it must be risky.* **Song, Hyunjin y Schwarz, Norbert.** s.l. : Psychological Science, 2008, PSYCHOLOGICAL SCIENCE.
58. *Predicting short-term stock fluctuations.* **Adam, L. Alter y Oppenheimer, Daniel M.** 2006, PNAS.
59. *Preference fluency in choice.* **Novemsky, Nathan, y otros, y otros.** No. 3, s.l. : Journal of Marketing Research, 2007, Vol. Vol. 44.

This book was sponsored by The Persuasion Institute of The Americas, an organization specialized on business and personal persuasion coaching; addressed to everyone who wants to improve their persuasive qualities in their messages.

- Negotiate with powerful psychological levers
- Convince and influence others in an effective way
- Sell ideas or anything else successfully
- Be free of manipulations

Information available at:

www.persuasion-institute.com